"There will be painful times when you have to say goodbye to people you really like who just do not get the mission or live its values. On days like those, you might wish your mission and values were vague and generic.

"They can't be. Take the time. Spend the energy. Make them real."

—Jack Welch
Winning

The
CORE VALUES
C🧭MPASS

Moving from
CYNICISM *to a*
CORE VALUES CULTURE

Dennis F. Haley

Academy Leadership Publishing

ISBN: 978-0-9727323-5-2

Library of Congress Control Number: 2009944211

Academy Leadership books are available at special quantity discounts to use as premiums and sales promotions, or for use in corporate training programs. For more information, please call Academy Leadership at 866-783-0630, or write to: 10120 Valley Forge Circle, King of Prussia, PA 19406.

Table of Contents

        By Robert A. McDonald
        CEO, Procter & Gamble Co.

INTRODUCTION

When the 82-year-old General Douglas MacArthur gave his farewell speech to the Cadet Corps at West Point in 1962, it would have been understandable if he had taken the occasion to tell some war stories and offer lessons from his experiences.

MacArthur had a lot to tell. He was a veteran of both world wars and the Korean War. He was the most highly decorated American officer of World War I. He was awarded the Medal of Honor for his defense of the Philippines in World War II. For more than five years he led the reconstruction of Japan's government and its economy.

Instead of recounting these experiences, though, MacArthur chose that day to tell the Cadet Corps about values. His now-famous speech is known by its simple three-word title: "Duty, Honor, Country." MacArthur told the cadets that those words "are your rallying point to build courage when courage seems to fail, to regain faith when there seems to be little cause for faith, to create hope when hope becomes forlorn." The future, he said, will be full of new challenges, along with many problems and controversies, but "your guidepost stands out like a tenfold beacon in the night: Duty, Honor, Country."

Here was a man who had participated in some of the great events of the 20th century. From his perspective after having lived 82 years, however, he saw that even the greatest events are transitory and fade from memory. Only values endure.

The business world has seen its share of great events these past few years, including the largest investment fraud of all time, the biggest corporate bankruptcy filing in U.S. history, and an ongoing succession of enormous loan write-offs. It is a turbulent time for even the healthiest of companies. Decentralization, mergers and acquisitions, technological change, and leadership turnover make it essential that companies have a clear purpose and values to serve as that "tenfold beacon in the night."

The words that describe a corporate purpose and values are important, but they are not sufficient. The executive leaders of any organization need to model behavior that reflects those values. They must ensure that the values are consistent and aligned with the organization's purpose and goals. Individuals at every level within the organization need to believe that their daily activities are helping achieve something meaningful. It's up to their leaders to grant them that focus so that the corporate values are expressed in observable behavior throughout the organization every day.

All this takes work, which is why it is so easy to be cynical about bringing corporate values to life. The job of focusing and aligning behaviors with values never ends, which leads some to question whether it's worth trying. Mergers, reorganizations, and restructurings make employees especially wary of being toyed with. And during times of great strain, it is tempting for leaders at every level to place short-term results and performance measures ahead of all other concerns, treating questions of corporate purpose and values as secondary issues.

What follows is the fictional story of one young leader who struggles with that very temptation as he leads his team through a difficult merger with the help of his *Core Values Compass*.

CHAPTER 1

The "Evil Empire" Encroaches

Guy Cedrick glanced at his watch as he stepped through the elevator doors in the darkened lobby. He had exactly nine minutes to make it to his boss's office for their 8:30 Monday morning meeting.

During the elevator ride, Guy braced himself for the predictable rituals of their weekly sit-down. He knew that J.W. Eaton, son of the founder of the Eaton Group, would start off by regaling him with the details of his weekend, which always seemed to involve the excruciating particulars of golf putts nearly sunk and deep-sea fish almost caught.

Then, once J.W. warmed to the subject of business, he'd talk about prospective clients—also in the vein of "the one that got away." Only then would Guy be able to dig into the dreary details of decisions that needed to be made. J.W. Eaton appeared to enjoy discussing his "almost" life a little more than the life he actually had.

The elevator doors opened on the fifth floor to reveal a silent unlit sea of unoccupied workstations. Guy walked across the room and into his own office, gathered some papers off his desk, and made his way to J.W.'s office.

On quiet mornings like this, it sometimes struck Guy what an unexpected course his young career had taken. Art history classes and playing linebacker for Penn State hadn't prepared him for running a marketing firm. Guy had majored in marketing, true, but he had always expected to work on the design side of the field. Not so long ago, his career goal was to become the art director at a mid-size firm, and to do some fine arts photography and painting on the side.

When Guy had started at the Eaton Group ten years earlier, he was an entry-level print designer, and the entire company employed just 15 people in a cramped converted loft space in Philadelphia's Old City section. Walter Eaton, the company founder, soon handed the firm over to his son, J.W., and that's when the growth began. J.W. kept acquiring smaller firms and bringing in new people until the once-little Eaton Group had nearly 120 employees and occupied a much larger office suite.

Ironically, J.W. Eaton had no real interest in any of those 120 people he had hired, so he kept handing Guy new managerial responsibilities. Guy's list of direct reports continued to lengthen until he was functioning as the *de facto* chief operating officer of a mid-size firm.

It was a position no one else wanted to fill. Ellen Grady, the tough-minded chief finance officer who was almost 15 years

Guy's senior, avoided talking to J.W. whenever she could. Although Ellen was a methodical marathon runner who rose at dawn and was always in training for her next race, even she lacked the patience to deal with J.W.'s shallow understanding of the business. And so, unwillingly, Guy had gradually become the go-between for his company's CFO and CEO.

It had been almost six years since Guy had drawn or designed anything at work. He hadn't run a marketing campaign in the past two. Instead, his days were now filled with managing other managers. As much as he missed the creative challenge of graphic design, though, he had come to see that leadership is an art form, too—one that's practiced on a much larger canvas than most.

Yes, there were the silly charades with J.W., and plenty of other aggravations that came along with his job, but Guy had decided years earlier that leadership is not just a responsibility, but also a choice. Obstacles and challenges are easier to bear once you accept them as your own. On the football field, he remembered, you look forward to facing the strongest opponents. You want to be tested, because that's how you improve.

Guy knew that adversity in business can help people and teams grow in similar ways, but over the years he had found that most people are too worried about their livelihoods to really embrace the idea. That's where he often felt his leadership could make a big difference. Guy took every opportunity to remind his Eaton Group colleagues how unforeseen problems and unexpected challenges would make them better and stronger. He had to work at reminding himself of that, too.

By 8:28, Guy had perched his 6-foot-3 frame on the edge of an armless chair in J.W.'s office. There was no way that J.W. would show up a second earlier than he had to, so Guy busied himself with paperwork while he waited. Lights began flickering on as other employees settled at their desks. The phones had just begun to ring when J.W. strode into the office.

Uncharacteristically, there were no fish stories this morning. Instead, J.W. looked around as if to ensure that no one was nearby, then shut the door to his office.

"Listen, Guy, I haven't told you this before, but I'm trying to swing a deal with Argosy," J.W. said excitedly as he sat behind his desk.

Guy tried to hide his surprise. Argosy Marketing and Advertising was one of the big downtown firms. J.W. had nicknamed the agency the "Evil Empire," and he regularly bemoaned Argosy's habit of courting Eaton Group clients. Secretly, Guy had always suspected that the problem wasn't so much Argosy's loose ethics as it was J.W.'s inability to keep clients happy. Not that he'd suggest that to J.W. himself.

"I'm pitching Ted Stone on having us go in together on some big bids," J.W. continued, running a hand through his professionally dyed hair. "We're talking about a strategic alliance, but it might be something more."

Guy thought he heard J.W.'s voice tremble at the word "more."

"Anyway, here's where you come in," J.W. said. "They want to meet you. Well, Ted Stone wants to meet you. He asked me to send you over tomorrow at two."

Guy blinked. He supposed this was how it felt to be blindsided. "How should I prepare for that?" he asked. "I mean, is there an account we're going after together?"

"No, we've got nothing specific to look at," J.W. replied, rocking back in his chair. "It's just a get-acquainted kind of thing. Ted likes our work, but he told me he wants to see who's really making the trains run on time over here. And I told him that's you."

Guy smiled. It might have been the nicest thing J.W. had ever said to his face. And it was definitely true. "So just go over there and tell him how you crack the whip," J.W. added. "This could be big. Really big." J.W.'s eyes took on a faraway look, as he no doubt imagined just how big a partnership with Argosy could be.

Guy brought J.W. down to earth with his next question. Although his boss had the luxury of daydreaming about what might happen, Guy had to deal with what actually *was* taking place.

"Everyone on the Concord Financial project is asking me about bonuses," Guy said. "I don't know what I should tell them." J.W. lowered his eyes and started walking toward his water cooler.

"Well, you're going to have to keep stringing them along about that," he replied without looking at Guy.

As J.W. filled his cup, he explained that although Concord loved the marketing program that Eaton Group had designed, the mortgage product had run into regulatory obstacles. Now Concord was debating whether to revamp the program or scrap it.

Guy grimaced. He could guess at what J.W. was hinting. If Concord's program was losing money, the company might want to share the pain with the Eaton Group. J.W. would have to discount Concord's fees, and then there would be no money left with which to reward the staff for their long nights and weekends of work.

"Don't go telling the staff about it," J.W. cautioned, taking a sip of water. "Just tell them we're still waiting to hear from Concord. In the meantime you and I have Argosy to worry about— but don't tell them about Argosy, either."

So much for transparency, Guy thought.

J.W. flicked open his cell phone, which signaled the end of the meeting. "You know," he said as Guy stood up and walked toward the door, "I would have sent you over to Argosy today, but I knew you wouldn't be wearing a suit."

He paused and looked up as Guy was leaving. "Wear a nice one tomorrow, okay?"

CHAPTER 2

Meetings and Mutterings

Guy normally spent Monday mornings making the rounds of Eaton Group department heads, except for business development, which he left to J.W. After checking in with the information technology people, it was time to review company finances with Ellen Grady.

"Hey, congratulations on the award," Ellen said with a smile as Guy walked in. The previous Friday night, the company had won a regional Webby award for the Concord Financial website. The local distinction put them in the running for a national competition.

"That's Dwight Jones's Webby," Guy replied, referring to Eaton Group's director of web design. "He did an amazing job on Concord. But you and he are running buddies, right? He must have told you all about it himself."

"Oh, we don't run together anymore," Ellen said with a shake of her head. "Dwight says he's way too busy. And I know it's not just Dwight carrying the Concord Financial project. I cash the checks around here. It's a big account."

"Funny you mention Concord," Guy said. "I've got a question. J.W. hinted this morning that their home mortgage program is in trouble and that we might get hurt as a result. Has Concord been paying its bills?"

Ellen looked sideways at Guy. "What did J.W. tell you?"

"He gave me the distinct impression that Concord is angling for a discount," Guy answered. "It was after I asked him about staff bonuses."

Ellen made a face. "Concord Financial is a public company," she said. "Do you think they want it to get around that they're stiffing their vendors?"

"So they're paid up?" Guy asked.

Ellen nodded. "It makes no sense for them to nickel and dime us," she explained. "They would look desperate and then their stock price might take a hit." Her blue eyes narrowed. "Did J.W. tell you they hadn't paid?"

"No, not exactly," Guy replied, drawing the words out. "But he did tell me that I should string along the staff about bonuses until we hear more from Concord. He made it sound like there was a problem, and that he was taking me into his confidence about it."

"Confidence is the key word, Guy," Ellen said with some sadness in her voice. Then she sighed. "He's conning you and everyone else. He just doesn't want to give the staff those bonuses."

Guy knew that Ellen was right. After all these years, he still felt a twinge of hurt feelings whenever he caught J.W. trying to mislead him. He turned and stared out the window as he thought about how narrow his boss's focus was. Didn't J.W. know that Guy would check his story with Ellen?

"I hope you're keeping your resume fresh," said Ellen. "Because I sure am."

Guy gave a hollow laugh and turned back around. "You'd leave me here alone with J.W.?"

Ellen didn't even smile. "I miss his father," she said. "I liked coming in when old Walter was in charge. We were a smaller company and there were no...shenanigans."

"That's for sure," Guy agreed. He didn't argue, but his memories of the Eaton Group in its struggling earlier days were not nearly as rosy as Ellen's. He recalled the firm being understaffed and under-equipped, and the staff underpaid. "We'll never see days like those again."

The last stop on Guy's morning rounds was with the department heads of the productive side of the firm—the Eaton Group's creative team.

The stated purpose of this weekly meeting was for everyone to share what they were doing and to ask for help across department lines. Guy was determined to make the meeting brief and useful, which was a constant challenge. He had set it for 11:30 so everyone would be hungry and eager to break for lunch.

Most of the department heads were already in the small conference room when Guy arrived. After he had greeted everyone,

Linda Hutchinson, head of multimedia production, started with a rundown of all the projects her group was handling. The staff was stretched thin, as usual, she said, and now they were having technical difficulties with some of the equipment, which might need repair.

"What can I do to help?" Guy asked.

"I'd like you to call someone in, but I'm afraid they'll shut us down if you do," Linda answered. "So I'm waiting for some downtime, but the equipment is slowing us up so much that I don't know when we'll get the chance to have it fixed."

Guy furrowed his brow. Clearly, Linda didn't want to make the decision. He would have to. He promised to sit down with her later and come up with a schedule for the repairs, and jotted down a brief reminder for himself.

Next, Andy Smythe, master of business-to-business programs and sales kit rollouts, ran down his list of projects. He needed help from Linda with a promotional DVD and asked Dwight Jones, the web design director, about some data entry glitches on one of the business-to-business websites.

After Andy had finished speaking, Randi Myers lost no time in distributing a huge packet of handouts, listing all the special events her crew was handling that month for Eaton Group clients.

"Are we supposed to go over all this now?" asked Dwight, crossing his arms.

Randi looked hurt. "This is just fun stuff we're doing around town, and I thought everyone might like to know about it," she replied, avoiding Dwight's slightly scornful look.

Trying to salvage the situation, Guy went out of his way to thank Randi for the report. He made a note to talk to her later, though, to remind her about the purpose of the meeting.

When it was Dwight's turn to speak, he waved at the stack of printouts he had brought with him and said, "It's just the same old, same old. What everyone's really wondering about is this rumor that we're going to be bought by Argosy."

Guy's mouth fell open, but no one else at the table seemed surprised. Wherever Dwight had gotten the rumor, he'd obviously already told everyone about it except Guy. Typical.

"I don't know what you're talking about," Guy hedged. In his mind, though, he played back J.W.'s comment that "It could be *more.*" Is this what J.W. meant? Was he really going to sell Eaton Group to Argosy?

"If you did know, would you tell us?" Dwight asked.

"Well, you've got me there," Guy said. Outwardly, he remained pleasant, but inside he was fuming. Dwight had raised the question only in order to bait him, and everyone at the table knew it. "But I can't say anything, because I don't know anything."

"Last week you said you'd find out about the Concord bonuses," Linda chimed in. "What's Wally got to say about it now?"

Wally was a derisive nickname for J.W., and Guy had explicitly asked the staff not to use it.

"Right now, *J.W.* tells me that the account is up in the air," Guy said in a surprisingly calm tone of voice. He decided to parrot J.W.'s line, but he took it only so far. "Until we know for sure that the next phase will happen, J.W. says he can't put aside any money for bonuses. I know that's not what you want to hear, but as far as I know, that's where it stands."

After the meeting broke up, Guy called Linda aside.

"All of a sudden he's Wally again?" Guy asked her. "We've been over this. We don't do name-calling here."

Linda was defensive. "He stood there and told us we would get bonuses!" She put her hands on her hips, her voice rising a bit. "If he can't manage to get money out of Concord, why is that our problem?"

For the moment, J.W.'s advice to Guy—to remain vague and string everyone along—didn't seem so bad.

"Look, I understand you're upset, but I won't lie just to placate everyone for the moment," Guy told her, walking out of the conference room. "I think J.W. overpromised on the bonuses and now he can't bring himself to write the checks. I've cautioned him about this kind of thing before, but he can't seem to help himself."

"And what about us being sold to Argosy?" Linda asked, walking alongside Guy as he headed toward the central group of workstations. "Are we really going to go to work for those people?"

"I truly don't know anything about that."

"And if you did...."

"No, no. Believe me. A deal like that is way above my pay grade," Guy chuckled.

"I guess I should go to Dwight if I want more details," Linda said, but she had a smile on her face.

"If you do, let me know what he tells you."

CHAPTER 3

Into the Lion's Den

The next morning, Guy signed in at the main desk of Argosy's office tower in Center City Philadelphia. With a visitor badge clipped to his jacket pocket, he rode to the 35th floor executive offices. He felt his ears pop as the elevator shot skyward.

First, Guy waited in an outer reception area by the elevator bank for ten minutes until Ted Stone's personal secretary, a svelte young brunette, came to get him. Then he sat in an overstuffed leather chair for another 15 minutes outside the twin oaken doors to Stone's inner sanctum. All in all, Guy found the whole process to be intimidating, although he made a conscious effort to appear relaxed and confident.

Finally, the large doors in front of Guy opened, and Guy was faced with a tanned, well-groomed man in his middle fifties. Ted Stone. Immediately, Guy recognized the leader of Argosy as the kind of ad man J.W. so desperately aspired to be. Guy was physically larger than Ted Stone, yet Ted somehow, by his manner and the sheer strength of his personality, seemed to occupy more space.

As Ted shook Guy's hand and ushered him into his sleek, well-appointed office, Guy understood exactly how minor league baseball players must feel before their first game in the big leagues began. Squaring his shoulders, he took a seat in the chair Ted Stone indicated.

"I finally got J.W. off the subject of his fishing boat," Ted began without preamble, sitting in the ergonomic leather chair behind his desk. "Then I managed to pry out of him what makes the Eaton Group tick. Among other things, he told me how much he relies on you to get projects out the door."

"I'm glad to hear that," Guy responded, both surprised and gratified by Ted's directness. "I don't always hear it directly from J.W."

"Acknowledgment. That's a communication thing, isn't it?" Ted said. "It's funny, about a year ago we had some consultants here to do what they call a 'visions and values' process. They did it first with the executive staff and then with everyone. And it was fascinating to me, because it turned out that communications in this company needed a lot of work. And we're in the communications business!"

Guy recalled an old saying his mother was fond of repeating. "The cobbler's kids go barefoot," he said.

"Precisely," Ted agreed. "So we went about this process to define the four things we value here more than anything: Respect, Integrity, Communications, and Excellence. And you know, I don't think there's a problem around here we can't solve, or at least make a dent in, if we go at it with those four core values in mind."

Ted leaned forward over his desk. "Let me ask you this: Does the Eaton Group have a purpose?"

Guy was sorely tempted to say something snide about keeping J.W.'s fishing boat maintained, but he bit his tongue. Bad-mouthing his boss was not the route he needed to take, especially after Ted had just brought up "core values." "A purpose?" he asked instead. "You mean like a mission statement?"

Ted Stone nodded.

"No, I can't say that we do," Guy admitted. "We just keep growing. J.W. jokes sometimes that our motto should be 'Eaton: Eat or be eaten.'"

"Not terribly stirring, is it?" Ted said with a smile. "But I'm not surprised. I think three out of four companies—big companies, I'm talking about—have never identified why they exist, except to make money."

He reached behind his desk to a large bookshelf and retrieved a three-ring binder. Its cover read, "Argosy: Introducing a world of new possibilities."

Ted studied Guy's face as Guy read the words aloud. "That's our purpose," Ted said with obvious pride. "We look at every project and ask ourselves, 'What's the new possibility here? What are we introducing into the world?' And then we go after it, with respect, integrity, communication, and excellence. That's in all our printed materials. It's on our website. It's even on the lunchroom wall. It's what we tell every new hire and every new client."

"That's very inspiring," Guy said politely. This was a lot to digest. He felt as though Ted had just disclosed the meaning of his life and was awaiting a response.

"And I tell our people," Ted continued, "that when they're bidding for a new client, if that client's not bringing some new possibility into the world, then maybe Argosy's not interested in the account."

"Wow," Guy said, genuinely surprised. "Have you really turned away clients that way?"

"No," Ted replied. "None so far, anyway. But we've talked about it." He shifted in his chair, then continued. "Guy, I know I'm coming on a little strong here, but I've got some important decisions to make, and I need some help from you. How well do you think this kind of stuff would go over with your team on Third Street? If we collaborate in some way, are they ready to play at this level? To be honest with you, I'm a little worried we'd just be speaking in different languages and end up making a big mess of things."

Guy could just imagine how talk of "visions and values" might draw cynical reactions from a few people in his creative team, but he didn't let on.

"I think that a lot of people would be grateful for the sense of direction," he said, carefully weighing his words. "That's just for starters. For others, well, you know, this is the marketing business. We've all got pretty sharp instincts about what's for real and what's just for show. Most of the key people at the Eaton Group will take their cues from their supervisors. I've had some personal experience with that."

Figuring that Ted would appreciate hearing the backstory behind his reasoning, Guy told the other man about how he had developed his own Personal Leadership Philosophy four years earlier. At that point in time, the Eaton Group was experiencing severe growing pains, and Guy's seat-of-the-pants leadership style had begun to fail him. He'd had to become more intentional as he led his staff forward. Because he had developed a clearly written list of his leadership beliefs, his expectations, and his personal hot button issues, Guy said, he felt that Eaton Group's employees had responded by meeting him more than halfway.

"Expectations are a basic courtesy to extend to employees, but I also thought it was important to list my hot buttons," Guy explained, feeling a bit of relief when he saw Ted nod. "They are gossip, whining, complaining, being late for meetings, and not admitting when you're wrong."

Most people at Eaton Group had responded very positively, he continued, though they were cautious at first. Afraid that he was beginning to sound boastful, Guy added, "I mean, there's some grumbling in every workplace, and a few people still don't get it, but these problems don't get out of hand like they used to."

Ted nodded again, and Guy stopped backtracking. He blinked as a flock of birds flew past Ted's large picture windows.

"I don't suppose J.W. has distributed a Personal Leadership Philosophy, has he?" Ted said in a teasing voice.

Guy grinned and deflected the jab. "No. But most of my creative team leaders have. And that's really made a difference. I can tell." It was true, too.

"Well," Ted said with smile, "to be fair to J.W., I haven't done anything like that, either."

Then Ted cleared his throat, and Guy felt a change in the room's atmosphere. Sure enough, the levity had fled right out of Ted's 35th floor windows.

"Guy, I need to be straight with you here," he said. "Partnering with the Eaton Group would help your company a lot more than it would help mine. If I wanted the benefit of your work, I'd prefer to just bring you all on board. And although I'd appreciate if you'd keep this a secret, J.W. and I are trying to arrive at a price to do just that."

For the second time in as many days, Guy felt blindsided. Dwight's rumor was more than just a rumor, after all. Guy could hardly believe his ears. "What, you'd bring us all downtown to work here?" he managed to say.

"No, no, no," Ted said with a smile, picking up a pen and rolling it between his fingers. "I'd want to leave you right where you are. You all would become a specialty marketing shop, run as a division of Argosy. All the other functions, the back office, the accounts management, IT, all that would be handled here."

Guy knew what that meant. Jobs disappear during buyouts and mergers. Ellen Grady and her people would be gone, along with most of the IT and business development folks.

He tried to focus his thoughts, even though they were spinning so furiously he was surprised his head remained still. "So J.W. would continue to run the Eaton Group under Argosy's ownership?"

"No, I'd want J.W. to come here and help handle clients," Ted responded just as his phone started buzzing. "Third Street would be *your* production house. You'd report to me, and our chief creative director. But for the most part, you'd be on your own."

Guy was dumbstruck. He wasn't sure if he'd just won the lottery or if he'd been handed a ticking bomb. "Wow," he finally stammered. "I really don't know what to say."

"You don't need to say anything now," Ted replied. "For now, we're just two guys talking."

The phone buzzed again, and Ted picked up on speakerphone mode. According to his assistant, there were five junior account executives waiting outside to see him. Ted stood, and Guy picked up on his cue that the meeting was finished.

Guy's head was swimming as he made his way to the door. "Thanks, Guy," Ted told him. "One way or the other, we'll see each other again soon. Here's hoping J.W. and I can work out a few of the details."

When the double doors opened, the young ad execs jumped to attention in the reception area. A few stared at Guy, assuming he might be someone important since he'd had a private meeting with Ted.

As Guy approached the elevator bank, he heard Ted's oaken double doors thump closed behind him. The sound seemed somehow fitting—as if one chapter in his professional life was being audibly demarcated from the entirely new one that lay ahead.

CHAPTER 4

On Captaining a Company

J.W. was nowhere to be seen back at the office. Guy was surprised by that—he'd have figured that J.W. would want to hear every detail of the meeting—but his boss's absence gave Guy the chance to spend the rest of the day lost in thought. He tried, with dubious success, to imagine the Eaton Group without an Eaton at the top.

Guy sighed, deciding that he needed a bit of perspective. Switching on his computer screen, he typed in Argosy's web address and re-read Ted Stone's biography, trying to ignore the power shot of Ted that dominated the top right-hand corner of the page's layout.

According to his biography, Ted had begun his career in ad sales and had then worked his way up to account executive at a large agency. He started his own little firm at the age of 34—Guy's age. Argosy itself was just ten years old, founded in a merger with a lot of borrowed money. That's how Ted Stone became a wealthy man.

"I chose the name Argosy," read a quote in the biography, "because life is a long journey, like the argosy taken in Greek myth by Jason and the Argonauts. The Golden Fleece they sought is an enduring symbol of everyone's hope for a better, brighter tomorrow."

Idealistic...I wonder if Ted really *means it or if he just thought it sounded good,* Guy thought as he switched his screen back off and resumed staring at an unexceptional spot on the opposite wall.

When he got home that evening, Guy decided to hold off on telling his wife, Melanie, about all of the meeting's details. Melanie had other things on her mind, anyway. She asked him twice if he'd gotten her messages at work. Giving her a perfunctory kiss on the cheek, Guy confessed that he hadn't checked his voicemail once.

"I need your help with something," Melanie explained, just as Guy began to head toward the stairs. "Donna is going to need braces this year, and I found a way we can save about $1,000 in taxes if you sign up at work for something called a health reimbursement account."

Melanie had worked as an accountant before their two children came along, and Guy trusted her to manage all of their household finances. Normally he would have been glad to listen to how she'd found a way to save them money, but the Ted Stone meeting had left him preoccupied, and the thought of dealing with tax forms irritated him.

"Do you have the paperwork?" he asked. He tried not to sound annoyed, and suggested she put the forms in his briefcase so he wouldn't forget to take them to work the next day. Then he headed back toward the basement, not even bothering to change out of the suit he'd worn specifically for the Ted Stone meeting.

"I've got to go talk to Stanley next door," Guy called over his shoulder as he descended the stairs. Somewhere in the basement was a tool that needed returning to Stanley's workshop. After four years of being the older man's neighbor, Guy still didn't like going to visit him empty-handed.

Stanley Sabato was a retired U.S. Navy captain. He had first mentored Guy in the ways of naval leadership years earlier, when Guy was struggling to get the Concord Financial project off the ground. It was Stanley who had coached Guy on writing a Personal Leadership Philosophy and advised him to distribute it to his team. Even so, Guy tried to avoid burdening Stanley with his problems, even though Stanley always seemed glad to be of help.

After rooting around in his toolbox for a few seconds, Guy grabbed a wrench that he was fairly sure belonged to Stanley, pulled open the basement door, and headed across the lawn. As Guy had hoped, Stanley was home. He immediately invited Guy into his study, which was decorated with pictures and mementos from his years in the Navy.

As soon as Guy finished explaining what had happened that afternoon at Argosy, Stanley quizzed him about Ted Stone. That was one thing Guy appreciated about his neighbor—Stanley didn't waste time on irrelevant details.

"It sounds like Ted's asking the right questions about his firm," Stanley said. "And he seems willing to admit what he doesn't know. My question is, what's got you so worried?"

Guy fell silent. Sure enough, Stanley had already arrived at the heart of the matter. Focusing his gaze on a picture of a much younger Stanley in a tropical setting, Guy loosened his tie and unbuttoned his top button. He hated to admit what he was about to say.

"I'm afraid I've gotten used to handling J.W.," Guy blurted out, still staring at the photo on Stanley's desk. "The thing about having a negligent boss is that you get to do things your own way. I've pretty much got J.W. figured out. Yesterday, it took me about ten minutes to catch him in a lie. I can read him like a book."

"Yeah, but as I recall, it's not a very interesting book," Stanley pointed out with a half-smile. "Not very deep."

"True enough, " Guy admitted, looking back up. "But to go from that to working for Ted Stone...." His voice trailed off. "Ted's intimidating. He's a legend to some people, you know?"

"And you don't want to work for a legend?" Stanley asked. "You don't want a boss you can learn from? I mean, when was the last time you learned anything from J.W.?"

Stanley had a point, but Guy wasn't ready to concede his position just yet.

"I'm just worried that all these years with J.W. haven't prepared me for Ted Stone," he explained. "And Argosy must have a dozen mid-level people with more experience than me. Some of them could run the Eaton Group with their eyes shut. Once I mess up, I'm afraid Ted will dump me and send one of his own people down to Third Street to clean up after me."

"Come on," Stanley teased. He hoisted his feet onto the low coffee table between himself and Guy. "What do we always say? All you can do is know yourself, know your stuff, and know your people. Ted Stone is a new person you need to get to know."

"I know J.W., and J.W. knows he needs me," Guy countered. He imitated his host and propped his feet up on the coffee table as well. "Ted Stone? To him, I'm just another cog that comes along with a new division."

Stanley nodded. "Maybe, but that name, Argosy, tells me something," he said. "An argosy is a fleet of merchant ships. Maybe Ted sees himself as the admiral of the fleet and you'd be one of his captains. Every admiral lives and dies by his captains."

Guy's eyes narrowed at this piece of information. "Ted says on his website that he named the company after the journey that Jason and the Argonauts made."

"It says that?" Stanley looked amused. "That's funny. That's a common misreading of the word argosy. But take it from an old Navy man: An argosy is a fleet of ships. It's right out of Shakespeare and *The Merchant of Venice*."

"I'm surprised no one ever told Ted," Guy responded. As always, he was impressed by the breadth of his neighbor's knowledge. Sure enough, he could see *The Complete Works of William Shakespeare* dominating a shelf of the bookcase behind Stanley. Funny how he'd never noticed that before.

"Maybe they're afraid to tell him," Stanley chuckled. "Or maybe they've told him and he doesn't care. Either way, it sure says something about Ted Stone, doesn't it? There's no lack of self-confidence there." Changing tacks, he asked Guy about the Argosy offices.

"They're pretty formal," Guy said. "Very corporate. Lots of leather and windows. They've got the firm's purpose statement and values plastered everywhere, even in the lunchroom. 'Argosy: Introducing the world to new possibilities.' Then, under it, 'Argosy Values: Respect, Integrity, Communication, and Excellence.'"

Stanley paused for a moment to take this in. "Posting a set of core values for everyone to see can be a very good thing," he said. "We have three core values in the Navy: Honor, Courage, and Commitment. You see those values posted everywhere on some bases. Officers learn to take the values pretty seriously, because they're useful leadership tools. Sometimes we'd take entire days, Values Days we called them, just to discuss one value and determine what that value truly meant to everyone on the boat."

Guy tried to picture hardnosed sailors sitting around debating the meaning of commitment. It was kind of like imagining the Philadelphia Eagles discussing the finer points of Plato's philosophy in the locker room.

"So here's another question about Ted Stone," Stanley said, breaking into Guy's daydreams. "What does he do with those values? Are they just nice words that make pretty wall decorations? Or does he really *live* those values? I mean, based on those four values, what kind of expectations does he set for his people at Argosy? You might want to ask around about that."

"Ted said the consultants told him that Argosy employees need to work on their communications," Guy said. "He thought that was ironic, since Argosy is a communications firm, but he didn't say what they're doing about it. Still, that shows some self-awareness."

"It sounds like it."

"So what else do you think I should do while I wait for the other shoe to drop?"

"Just remember your Leader's Compass," Stanley said. "You're coming up on rough seas, no doubt. Use your compass to keep your bearings. Re-read your Personal Leadership Philosophy and make sure you're sticking to it."

Guy's face brightened. He felt greatly relieved by Stanley's practical advice. "Well, thanks, Stanley," he said. "That's something I can get my arms around."

"If you do become a part of Argosy, think about bringing your staff along with those four values," Stanley said, pointing his index finger at Guy. "Maybe you should hold your own Values Day. Then you'd be more likely to get buy-in from everyone at the Eaton Group. Instead of having the values dictated to them by Argosy, they'd get to sort out what the values look like for themselves. I could give you some pointers."

"That sounds great, if we can ever find the time to do one," Guy responded. "Were they really worth it to you? Could you see the difference in how your crew behaved afterwards?"

"You see some changes at first," Stanley acknowledged. "The real improvement comes later, after the values have been tested a few times."

"They watch to see if you practice what you preach, huh?"

"Yes, but it's more than that," Stanley said. He returned his feet to the floor and leveled his gaze at Guy. "It's not enough for a leader to live the values. You'll have to enforce them and defend them. When someone on your staff violates one of the core values, right out in the open, everyone else will wait to see how you respond. That's the test. They will want to know what these values really count for. At that point, your leadership is on the line. If you blow that call, a hundred more Values Days won't patch the hole in your credibility."

Stanley reached over to his desk for his laptop while Guy digested that particular piece of information.

"Respect, Integrity, Communication, and Excellence," Stanley muttered under his breath. "Hmm. Spells RICE. It's got a familiar ring to it." He booted up the laptop and started a web search.

"Know your people," Stanley intoned, sounding remarkably like a tie-bedecked corporate executive, a persona that was at odds with his no-nonsense buzz cut and weathered features. "You've got to take Ted Stone's measure and decide whether he's just another J.W. in slicker packaging."

Stanley pecked away at the laptop keyboard. "For now, Ted says he's ready to challenge you and your team to step up and play at a higher level," he continued. "What if you take him at his word? Maybe he's for real. Would that be so bad?"

Guy admitted that wouldn't be a bad thing at all.

Stanley's laptop screen revealed the search results. "Hah! I knew I'd seen those same four values somewhere before," he said with some satisfaction. "Guess who held up 'Respect, Integrity, Communication, and Excellence' as its core values?"

Guy had to admit he was curious.

"Who?" he asked.

Stanley smirked.

"Enron!"

Under New Management

It was a bright Wednesday afternoon when Guy returned to Third Street from a lunch meeting. He was just in time to see two workmen bolting a sign into the corridor wall. The sign read:

Eaton/Argosy:
Respect. Integrity. Commitment. Excellence.

Dwight Jones was leaning against the wall, idly supervising the installation while nursing a cup of coffee. It had been a month since the ownership change, and the pace of work in the office had slowed. There was a sense of calm before the storm.

"It's a little Big Brother-ish don't you think?" Dwight said to Guy. He gestured at the sign.

Guy pretended to be amused, although he had a feeling Dwight hadn't been joking. "Now you've made me curious, Dwight. Tell me, what do you find Orwellian about respect and integrity?"

"Nothing, of course," Dwight said, crossing his arms. "It's just that having those words right in your face every day is a little oppressive. They're so hollow. And they mean something different to everyone, don't they?"

"I don't know," Guy ventured, leaning his shoulder on the wall alongside Dwight. "I think I know when I'm being disrespected. And I think I know when someone I'm dealing with has integrity. Those two seem pretty clear to me."

Guy stopped there, though, before his little speech morphed into a full-fledged lecture. *Know your people*, he reminded himself.

Dwight was almost five years older than Guy, but Guy was the boss. The two had fallen into a pattern of passive-aggressive power struggles with each other, mainly because of Dwight's arrogant, high-handed manner with his office mates. During busy times of the year, Guy and Linda found themselves strategizing over about how to handle Dwight in hopes of preventing one of his infamous blow-ups.

But they never questioned whether Dwight was worth the trouble. He was responsible for every design award the Eaton Group had ever won. And he knew it.

"What about communication, though?" Dwight asked, lightening up a little. "That's tricky, don't you think? How is it a value? We all communicate. And excellence? What does that mean? Isn't that just in the eye of the beholder?"

"You may be right," Guy replied, nodding agreeably. But it was a strain. He was itching for the conversation to end so that he could return to the sanctuary of his office.

"Speaking of communication," Dwight continued, "Ellen says she hasn't heard from you."

Guy felt a twinge of guilt. It had been three weeks since Ted Stone had let her go, as she had expected he would. Guy hadn't found time to call and catch up with her, although he'd honestly meant to.

"Oh, she's fine," said Dwight. "But you should call her. You'll find out what these Argosy people are like once they've got no use for you." Dwight was again offering bait, and Guy vowed not to take it. "Yeah, this 'respect and integrity' gang in their Italian suits really gave her the shaft."

"I think she may be better off without them, don't you?" Guy countered. He fiddled with his BlackBerry to avoid Dwight's gaze, and was both surprised and gratified to see he had received a text message. The screen read:

G-

Call me.

Ted

"It's Ted. Gotta go."

"His master's voice," Dwight muttered, just loud enough for Guy to hear it.

Chapter 6

A "Camel" Campaign Commences

Twenty minutes later, Guy emerged from his office with a big grin on his face. He turned to Sonia, his fresh-out-of-college assistant, and asked her to gather all of the creative team department heads into the conference room right away. Then he asked her to send out for coffee and danishes.

"This is really exciting," Guy began once the group was assembled. "I just got off the phone with Ted Stone. They've got a national advertising campaign they want to roll out in less than six months, and we've got the marketing and public relations side of it all to ourselves."

"What's the product?" Linda asked. Guy knew that Linda's reaction was going to be important. As head of multimedia production, she would play an integral role in the upcoming campaign.

"Disposable cell phones!" Short of doing a pencils-on-table drum roll, Guy tried to make the big reveal as exciting as he could. He was genuinely thrilled, but all he got back were blank stares.

Except for Dwight, that is. Dwight looked disgusted. "Like the phones that crooks and spies use when they don't want to be traced?" he asked in a sarcastic tone, swiveling slightly back and forth in his chair. Everyone laughed.

"No, no, nothing like that," Guy replied, not betraying the twinge of annoyance he felt. "Look, every year one out of four cell phones gets lost, stolen, or damaged beyond repair. It's a multi-billion-dollar problem."

"I've dropped two in the toilet!" Randi chirped. Everyone laughed again. "Oh, and I laundered one, too."

"Okay, so we've got to get Randi one of these phones right away." Guy was glad to see the group smiling. He could have hugged Randi for drawing everyone's attention away from Dwight.

"One of the big cell phone carriers is behind this," he explained. "CellMobile has started up a new company called Trek-Phone. It's going to charge less for a disposable phone than what millions of people already pay just for cell phone insurance. It's really brilliant."

"So, what are they? Crummy little phones you can just throw away?" Now it was Linda who was skeptical.

"No, no, they're colorful and cool and fun," Guy countered.

Fortuitously, Sonia walked in at that exact moment with a couriered folder containing printout images of the TrekPhone.

Guy held up one of the pictures, and passed it around the table.

"This is a case of Ted Stone thinking big," Guy said. "He told me he worked hard for this account because he thinks this is where the whole cell phone industry is going. We're all accustomed to disposable pens, disposable lighters, and disposable razors. Ted predicts disposable cell phones are next, and we'll be right at the cutting edge."

He paused for dramatic effect. *Now to roll out the big guns,* he thought.

"But here's what's really great for us," Guy continued. "This new company, TrekPhone, is being run just like a lot of the start-ups we work with. They've got lots of energy, lots of drive, and they're totally committed to doing something that's never been done before. But, unlike all the other start-ups, TrekPhone has big bucks behind it. It's got CellMobile money—tons of it. So if we think we need more cash in the budget to do something right, and we're ready to make a case for it, the money is there!"

"So when do we meet with them?" Linda asked. She sounded mollified, and, Guy hoped, maybe even a bit eager.

He paused again, for a different reason. "We don't. Not now, anyway."

"Then how do we get started?" Linda looked puzzled, as did several other faces around the table.

"Ted says they have the advertising campaign already sketched out over at Argosy," Guy explained. This was the part his team wasn't going to like. "They want us to do the marketing off their lead."

"Without any of our input?" Andy was incredulous.

Dwight rocked back in his chair. He looked up at the ceiling and recited in a pompous tone of voice, "Respect. Integrity. Communication. *Excrement.*" Everyone laughed, including Guy.

"Okay, Dwight," Guy said. "I admit, Argosy hasn't handled this in an ideal way. I'm not happy about it, either. But this is the kind of campaign we never got a chance to do before the merger. Let's try to write off the poor communication from Argosy as just part of a rocky transition. I'd like us all to pull together and prove to Argosy that this creative team can take any handoff and run with it."

Guy's inspirational moment was greeted only by worried looks. Hardly the response he'd hoped for.

"But they already have the advertising concepts nailed down!" Now it was Kate the writer's turn to whine. "What if we don't like what they've done? How do we work around that?"

"They're giving this to us because they're trusting us to do what we do best," Linda jumped in. She was trying to rally to Guy's side. "Even if we need to break with the theme of their advertising, right?" She sounded hopeful. Guy grimaced.

"I already talked to Ted about that," he admitted. "He wants us to work from the ad campaign. 'Make it work,' he said. I know you all can do it."

There was a knock on the conference room's door, prompting Guy to breathe a silent sigh of relief. The coffee and danishes had arrived, and he was grateful that they momentarily deflected the room's attention from him.

After everyone had helped themselves to the refreshments, Guy passed around more of the Argosy printouts that Sonia had brought in. They looked like finished advertising prints and storyboards for TrekPhone television and multimedia spots.

Everyone had to admit that the ad copy was clever enough. One was titled, "Talk Is Cheap." Another was called "Get the Message," because the TrekPhone offered instant text messaging. The third theme was "All Backed Up." TrekPhone would use CellMobile's network and would save data to each user's personal website instantly, so information was backed up if the phone was ever lost.

"Let's get the goal clear here," Guy ventured. "Our job is to create the marketing materials off these ads. We want to get this phone into convenience stores, pharmacies, and other places where consumers make impulse buys."

"But that's a business-to-business approach," Andy complained, crumpling up his napkin. As the team member in charge of business-to-business campaigns, he was skeptical. "What I see here is a consumer ad campaign. It's apples and oranges."

"Ted Stone says it's not." Guy was adamant. "He thinks a good consumer ad campaign will drive the business-to-business sales. Retailers will want to carry the phone because they'll like these ads as much as anyone."

Andy stared down at the ads. He seemed unable to say anything more.

"Let's try and stay positive," Guy began to wrap up. "Linda, I've already asked you to lead the first big project we get from Argosy, so here it is."

Dwight rose from his seat and gave Linda an exaggerated high-five with feigned exuberance. Everyone else did the same, mimicking Dwight as they filed out the door.

Linda sat there looking at Guy, every bit as amused as she always was when Guy's enthusiasm had been punctured. "You know," she said, her serious tone at odds with the smile that still lingered on her face, "the CellMobile backing sounds really good. And the ads are great-looking. But this marketing campaign could easily turn out to be a gigantic camel."

Guy nodded his head. "A horse designed by a committee, right?"

"You got it." She stood up and gathered her papers. "Ugly as heck and a lousy bet to win the Preakness."

"You really think it's that bad?"

"Most of it is okay," Linda admitted. "I can see how 'All Backed Up' is a funny double-entendre for selling cheap phones to the under-thirty crowd. But then if we use that same phrase in business-to-business materials aimed at pharmacies, what will they think? That this is a phone that comes with laxatives?"

Guy smiled. He could see some other pitfalls in Argosy's approach that he wasn't about to bring up.

"I don't know," Linda continued. "Maybe I'm making too much of it. I'm just not used to working this way."

She looked at Guy for a long moment. "Can't you go to Ted and tell him that Argosy might be wrong on this? Maybe you can ask him to give us a couple of weeks to pitch our own approach. If this does turn out to be a mess, it doesn't sound like we'll have time for a do-over."

"Let's try to stay positive," Guy said. "A camel won't win the Preakness, that's true. But what if you put one in the race? It would get a lot of attention, wouldn't it?"

After Linda left, Guy sat alone in the conference room for a minute. For years, he had been able to convince J.W. Eaton of just about anything. But Ted Stone? You either gave Ted Stone what he wanted, or he would find someone else who would. This was Guy's first project as head of Eaton/Argosy, and he could already see a wide no-man's-land between the two company cultures.

One thing was for sure: He had his work cut out for him.

TrekPhone Trouble

Before the end of the day, Argosy had sent over a sample TrekPhone for Guy to try out, and he made a few test calls during the drive home. Guy liked the phone's design. It was light and felt good in his hand. The buttons clicked reassuringly. The phone didn't have a great battery life, but the sound was clear and the ring was loud. All in all, not a bad package for a disposable product.

Once Guy and Melanie finished preparing dinner that night, they sat down with their two daughters. Guy handed the Trek-Phone to Donna, who had just turned seven.

"This is a great idea," Guy said to Melanie as Donna turned the phone over in her spaghetti sauce-spattered hands. "In a few years, I'd love to give her a cell phone and not be afraid that she'll lose it. Look at her, she's almost old enough to use it now."

Donna was hitting the buttons randomly, trying to peck out a tune.

"So tell me again why marketing is going to be such a problem with this thing?" Melanie asked.

"It shouldn't be," Guy said. "But there's already an us-versus-them vibe in the office. Argosy just dumped the job on us, and it's not the way we're used to working. Andy shocked me at today's meeting. I've never seen him so negative. The others seemed resentful, too, which is a shame, because this is an incredible project."

"Do they all think you should have handled things differently with Ted?" Melanie asked over the sounds of cell phone buttons that were still coming from the other side of the table.

"That might be part of it," Guy admitted. "Still, I'm surprised by the strong reaction. I thought I knew everyone better than this."

"There's been a big change," Melanie pointed out. "Your team is part of a large company now. Some of them probably had no intention of ever working for Argosy. Didn't you used to call Argosy the Evil Empire?"

"It's different, that's for sure." Guy examined an ice cube in his drink. "Ted Stone is a results-oriented guy. He says he likes debate and feedback. But he doesn't want it from us, not now." He sighed, then stood up and began clearing the table. "I feel like we're a new sports car to him. He wants to take us for a spin and see what we can do."

"When you talk about Ted Stone, he sounds like a very demanding client," Melanie responded, following Guy into the kitchen with a handful of plates. She could almost always put her finger on what was really bothering her husband. "But Ted is also your new boss, so you can't manage his expectations the way you would with a client. That's confusing."

"You're right," Guy agreed. "I'm confused; everyone's confused. None of us know how to take marching orders like this."

"What are you going to do?"

Guy considered the question. "I was thinking about something Stanley told me about the Navy, how they would sometimes hold Values Days for an entire crew."

"Value Days? That sounds like a sales promotion at Mega-Mart." Melanie hoisted two-year-old Molly into her arms and headed upstairs to run Molly's bath water.

"Very funny," Guy said. "It's *Values* Days, with an 's.' Stanley says he and his submarine crew would regularly take a whole day, a Values Day, to discuss the meaning of one of the Navy's core values. When he first told me about it, I thought it might be something worth trying later in the year, when things slow down a little."

He raised his voice as Melanie disappeared upstairs. "Now I'm thinking the TrekPhone campaign is liable to crash and burn unless we have a Values Day right away. I've got to do something to help pull everyone together. Sweet-talking them today didn't work. It won't work."

As he finished loading the dishwasher and wiping down the table, Guy considered all of the opposition he was likely to encounter if he planned a Values Day. For a few individuals in particular, the idea was likely to go over like the proverbial lead balloon.

Throwing the dishrag into the sink, he turned to Donna, his seven-year-old. "Sweetie, I need to call Stanley next door. Where's the pretty phone I gave you?" Donna shrugged, unconcerned, and went back to preparing her baby doll for bed.

"Hey, Guy," Melanie called from upstairs. "Can you come here a minute?" She was shouting over the din of running bath water.

"One second!" He started up the stairs, pausing for a few seconds to scan the living room floor for a glimpse of the Trek-Phone. It was gone.

Guy approached the bathroom and craned his neck around the door. Molly was in the tub playing "boats." The TrekPhone was bobbing in the water near her toes. It was decorated with bubble bath suds.

"Sorry," Melanie said sheepishly. "It's disposable, right?"

Guy had to smile. "I wonder if the TrekPhone people know that it floats?"

Values Day Finds Its Voice

The following Friday, Guy arrived at the office half an hour early to prepare for Eaton/Argosy's very first Values Day. Dwight Jones was already there, pecking at his keyboard in the thin morning light. Deciding that it wasn't too early for the team effort to begin, Guy asked Dwight to help him clear a space in the middle of the main room and fill it with folding chairs. To Guy's mild surprise, the other man pitched in immediately. Dwight was small and wiry, but as he handled the folding chairs Guy noticed for the first time how strong he was for his size.

The Values Day announcement memo had asked everyone to be prompt, and to Guy's pleasant surprise, the entire staff of Eaton/Argosy was present and accounted for by 9 a.m. Forty-five people stood around with coffee and bagels, stealing occasional glances at Guy and then at the clock. Guy waited until exactly 9:15, the promised start time, and then walked over to a desk near the far wall.

Whenever Guy stood up straight to address an audience, he noticed that the people in front often leaned back and crossed their arms. It was an unconscious, defensive posture, and Guy realized that his size could be intimidating. So now he always looked for a desk or a chair back to perch on, just to make his 6-foot-3 bulk appear a little more compact. He was more comfortable that way, too.

"We've got a big challenge in front of us," Guy began, calling the group to attention. "You all know about the TrekPhone campaign we've just been given, and you know that it's going to demand a new level of teamwork from all of us. So I'd like to start by discussing teamwork. What do we really know about it? Who wants to guess, for instance, where the word 'team' comes from?"

All sorts of suggestions came forth in rapid succession, most referring to team sports. Then someone called out, "Horse teams!"

"Right!" Guy acknowledged. "Teams of horses. That's at the root of the word. You harness these huge animals together and train them to pull in the same direction. That's how farmwork got done for centuries, until the tractor came along. But we're not beasts of burden, and the TrekPhone account is not an alfalfa field. We're thinking, creative human beings. So how do we get anything done as a team? What keeps us bridled and pointed in the same direction so we can achieve something together?"

Guy felt 45 pairs of eyes staring at him, but no one ventured an answer.

"Seriously. I'm asking. How does anything ever get done?"

"Cooperation?" It was Charlotte, a young staff writer who had been with them for only six weeks. "I mean, the team of horses doesn't understand why they need to pull the plow. But a team of people can cooperate because everyone understands the goal."

"Cooperation is important," Guy said, glad that Charlotte had broken the ice. "Very important. But what makes you cooperate with Kyle or Sam over there?"

"Money?" Charlotte's voice rose so timidly on the word that the room exploded in laughter. Guy felt relieved. His football instincts told him the crowd was now into the game. Maybe this Values Day wouldn't be as bad as he'd feared, after all.

"Money!" he exclaimed. "Of course! How many of us would have come in today if yesterday I'd sent around an email that read, 'We are now an all-volunteer workplace?' I don't see any takers."

More laughter.

"Okay," Guy continued. "So money matters. But your pay is what you get for doing what's in your job description and in the employee manual. What makes you a part of a *team*?"

"Leadership." It was Linda Hutchinson. To Guy's delight, she was actually taking notes on a legal pad.

"Good," Guy responded, nodding. "Team leaders help us cooperate. And most of your team leaders here have given you written copies of their Personal Leadership Philosophies. So when it comes to team leadership, just about everyone here should know what to expect, and what's expected of them."

"I haven't finished my PLP yet," squeaked Randi. Guy almost chuckled at the incredibly worried expression on her face.

"We still don't have every team leader's PLP, that's true," he said, holding up a hand. "But we won't worry about that now."

Guy tried to avoid looking at Dwight. For reasons that were very different from Randi's, Eaton/Argosy's webmaster had not written a PLP, and Guy assumed he never would.

"So far we've got leadership," Guy said, moving the conversation on. "We've got money, and we've got cooperation. Now, what's the last crucial thing we need as a team to keep us pulling in the same direction?"

"Values!" It was Charlotte again, all traces of timidity gone.

"Yes, values," Guy said. The room broke into applause. "This is why we're having Values Day. All of the other things we've mentioned are so much more obvious to us in the course of a regular day. It's easy to see people being cooperative. You can see when your paycheck hits your bank account. And we all look to our supervisors, our team leaders, for direction.

"But what about values? Even if we give common names to what we value most, how do we know if we agree with our teammates about what those values look like in action? Someone might call me Mr. Cedrick out of sincere respect, but I might wonder why he's being so cold and formal with me."

Guy was really warming to his topic now, and he could see several heads nodding throughout his audience. "So what are the behaviors that signify respect at Eaton/Argosy? What common idea of excellence do we hold here, so we all know it when we see it? Today I'm going to ask you all to take the four Argosy core values and determine what they look like for us, for this workplace, for the 46 people at Eaton/Argosy."

Guy looked slowly around the room. He made eye contact with as many people as possible.

"Each one of you is an important part of the shared culture here. I think that if we can join together and write down the common notions of what behaviors best express our shared values, then we can all live those values while we're here. And we can really work together as a team.

"For instance, I want to acknowledge everyone for showing up on time today," he said. "I would say that you did it as a matter of respect. You demonstrated respect for my request that you be on time. The fact that you *all* did it suggests to me that you share this fundamental value. So I'll just put that out there. Here at Eaton/Argosy, we would all agree that being on time for meetings is one way to live the core value of respect. Being on time is what respect looks like."

Guy paused to take a swig from his bottled water. Here was the part he had been looking forward to the most.

"Speaking of time, I am sure that a good number of you suspect this day is a big waste of time. I mean, we've got this giant project hanging over our heads. The clock is ticking on the TrekPhone launch. And here we are, taking a day out of our production schedules—a day we will never get back—to talk about touchy-feely values. Don't think I'm not aware of how strange this seems! So let me tell you why I felt we needed to talk about values today, before we get any deeper into the TrekPhone project.

"I got the idea for Values Day from my neighbor, Stanley Sabato. A few of you have met him. Stanley is retired from the Navy. He used to be the captain of a nuclear submarine, the USS Nevada. And he told me that they used to hold Values Days on a regular basis to talk about the Navy's core values—Honor, Courage, and Commitment.

"You know why Captain Sabato did that? Because when you are leading 140 men in a submarine hundreds of feet below the ocean's surface, teamwork is a life-or-death proposition. If certain teammates have a misunderstanding, everyone on board can end up as fish food in a manner of minutes. One mistake here, one mistake there, and they don't lose a client. They don't lose their jobs. They lose their lives."

Guy had his audience right where he wanted them. Bagels and coffee were forgotten, pens had stopped scribbling, and 45 pairs of eyes were trained on their leader.

"We're not in a life-or-death situation here," Guy told them. "We have the luxury of making mistakes and learning from them. But we have been drafted into service, in a way, by Argosy Advertising and Marketing. We're still the Eaton Group, but now Argosy is our lead horse. If we're going to succeed as a team, harnessed to Argosy, we have to pull in the same direction as Argosy. And that means that in our own way, we need to try and make Argosy's values our own."

Guy gave a nod to his assistant, who was positioned at the back of the room. "Sonia is passing out sheets of paper that assign each of you to one of four groups. With your group members, you'll go off in separate rooms, and each group will work on one of the four Argosy core values." He recited them slowly. "Respect. Integrity. Communication. Excellence.

"Argosy and its consultants have already defined these values in general terms. You see them here in your new employee manuals." Guy held one of the booklets up and read from it. "Excellence, for instance, is defined as 'Being the best and always striving to improve.'

"I'd like each group to come up with a long list of answers to this one fundamental question: What does this core value look like? I've already given you a start with what 'respect' might look like. It looks like being on time for meetings. What other evidence of respect would you like to see from your teammates here at Eaton/Argosy? Try to come up with a list that represents the consensus in your room. We'll meet back here in 45 minutes."

CHAPTER 9

A Disconcerting Discovery

Once everyone had disappeared into separate rooms in the building, Guy pulled out his BlackBerry to check his messages. He saw that he had missed a call from Melanie, so he decided to return it while he waited for the groups to return.

"Guy, did you remember to file that health reimbursement form, the one for Donna's braces?" Melanie asked after the obligatory "hellos." Instantly, Guy pictured the forms, still sitting in his briefcase.

"Oh, gosh, Honey, I completely forgot."

The line was silent on the other end. "I think it might be too late for this tax year now."

"I'll look into it," Guy promised, but his mind was still very much engaged by what his four groups were talking about. He began to walk around the perimeter of the common area, which was bordered by cubicles and workstations. "I know you said it was a thousand-dollar tax deduction, but it slipped my mind.

Today's a big day, and I don't feel like worrying about it right now, okay?" Melanie was quiet. "Okay," she finally said.

Guy told his wife that he loved her and apologized once more. Then, just as he was hanging up, something on Dwight's computer screen caught his eye. It was Ellen Grady's online resume.

Guy didn't feel entirely comfortable with what Dwight would surely see as an invasion of privacy, but curiosity got the better of him. He stepped into Dwight's cubicle and looked at the address bar on the screen. It was filled with developer code. Guy frowned. Dwight wasn't just visiting Ellen's site at work. He was *building* Ellen's site at work.

Although he could practically feel his blood pressure rising, Guy tried to stay cool as he called Ellen's cell phone. It was easy enough to do—he just had to read her number off Dwight's screen.

"Hey, Ellen, it's Guy. How are you doing?" Guy asked as he stepped out of Dwight's cubicle. He tried to keep his tone light.

"Guy, it's good to hear from you!" Ellen was clearly surprised to hear from Guy.

"Do you miss us?"

"Everyone but J.W. How's he doing at the Evil Empire?"

Guy flinched unconsciously. He'd been trying to squelch that particular epithet for what seemed like years now. "I don't know. I may see him when I go over to Argosy for lunch tomorrow."

"I remind myself that every day I don't have to deal with his cluelessness is a good day." Ellen chuckled, but Guy couldn't make himself wait any longer. He braced his free hand against a windowsill.

"Ellen, I need to ask you something. Is Dwight Jones designing a website for you?"

For a few seconds, there was silence on the other end of the phone. "Did he tell you he was?" Ellen sounded tentative.

"No, uh, someone else did," Guy hedged. He couldn't exactly admit that he'd just been snooping.

"Well, I hope it's okay with you," Ellen replied. "I know that Dwight does some design work on the side from home, and he offered to do it for me for nothing. But I insisted on paying him. He's not in trouble for this, is he?"

"Of course not," Guy said, watching pedestrians navigate the street below. "What he does on his own time, in his own home, is none of my business. I just wanted to make sure you knew how busy he is. I hope he hasn't promised to get it done for you too soon, because we are really hopping here."

Guy pushed off the windowsill and made his way back to Dwight's desk as he steered the conversation back into lighter territory. As he and Ellen said goodbye and promised to keep in touch regarding Ellen's job search, Guy stared at Dwight's desk. It had the usual cubicle décor: a framed picture of Dwight's Border Collie mix, a stress ball, and an African violet. There was also a stack of business cards on the desk—for something called

"DJDesign." Now, that definitely *wasn't* "the usual." And it certainly wasn't good.

Rift in the "Respect" Group

Apparently, time flies when you're brooding. Sooner than Guy expected, the teams returned from their four rooms, and the central office space filled with animated laughter and loud conversation.

To Guy's eye, three of the four groups were noticeably energized by the process. But the group with Dwight Jones in it, the one assigned the value "respect," seemed worn out. Some group members looked irritable, and no one was laughing.

"Respect" was first on his list for review, but Guy made a snap decision to skip it. Instead he asked the group assigned "integrity" to read from its list.

A web developer named Jackie stood up.

"Jackie, would you please tell us how Argosy defines 'integrity'?" Guy asked. "Now remember, this is the definition that Argosy and its consultants arrived at last year. Again, we're working from Argosy's definitions all day, but we decide which behaviors fit those definitions here at Eaton/Argosy."

Jackie read aloud: "Integrity. Upholding professional ethics. Keeping commitments to ourselves, our colleagues, and our clients."

"Okay, Jackie," Guy said. "Now, would you read us what your group came up with?"

She flipped open a spiral-bound notebook.

"We practice what we preach.

"We underpromise and overdeliver.

"We are ethical.

"We don't make false promises to make people feel better.

"We keep our promises or tell people as soon as we know we can't.

"We accept outside criticism."

Guy felt encouraged—the "integrity" group had taken its assignment seriously. He asked the whole room for more suggestions. Almost as soon as he asked the question, someone proposed, "We don't lie."

Others wondered if that fell under "We are ethical."

Raising a hand to quiet the discussion, Guy announced, "I have a problem with 'We are ethical.'" A few people laughed, which then caused the whole room to erupt. Guy laughed with them.

"Okay, that came out wrong," he said. "I support being ethical. But what does that look like? You can see someone keeping a promise, but can you see someone 'being ethical'? How about this: 'We will ensure that our actions are ethical and legal.' That way we're promising to take action, to get better at understanding our professional ethics. It's a small change, but I think it matters."

Sure enough, heads nodded. "So, why don't we go ahead and examine 'ethical'?" Guy asked, taking advantage of the natural segue.

After a productive discussion on the Eaton definition of ethics, followed by a coffee break, the session continued with the group assigned to "communication." The Argosy definition was, "We seek to understand and seek to make ourselves understood." And that's when things started to go south.

"I don't think communication belongs in a list of values," Dwight said to the room at large before the group leader had even had a chance to read his team's suggestions. "I understand how we want integrity and excellence and respect, but communication can mean just about anything. And there's such a thing as too much communication, you know? I mean, if we're all communicating all the time, how does any work get done?"

Guy wore a smile on his face like a frozen mask. "Okay," he said. "Anyone else?" He hoped that someone would offer a more constructive comment and draw attention away from Dwight's negativity.

Charlotte—too young and idealistic to know what she was about to get into—volunteered. "I don't think you can have enough communication. That's how we all stay together as a team and cooperate. If we don't communicate, how can we know how to help each other?"

Dwight looked disgusted. Before Guy could cut him off, the other man leaned back and shot a withering glare in Charlotte's direction. "*Obviously*, we have to communicate," he retorted. "I don't know what you heard me say. I certainly didn't say that we should never communicate. Learn to listen, okay?"

There was shocked silence in the room. Everyone was looking at Guy, waiting to see how he would handle the situation. Dwight was staring at him, too. Guy had a good idea of how he'd *like* to handle the situation, but it certainly wasn't appropriate for a meeting on values.

"Let's not make this personal, okay?" Guy said, trying not to say something he would regret. "This can be difficult stuff to get through. Now what was that we just saw? I would say we saw a mis-communication over the importance of communication."

A few people giggled nervously, doing very little to dispel the tension. "So thank you, Charlotte, and you too, Dwight. This is not easy."

The "respect" group was last, and the interchange between Dwight and Charlotte had set it up.

"We had a few problems in there," Andy said, standing up to relay his group's views.

I'll bet you did, thought Guy.

"Respect," Andy began, "is defined by Argosy as 'We treat everyone as an important and valued person.'"

"Look, here we go again," said Dwight. Guy could practically feel the room's temperature drop. "This list...."

Guy interrupted, his smile mask intact. "We haven't heard the list yet." He motioned to Andy to continue.

Andy began to read:

"Treat each other with dignity.

"Say only good things about our people.

"Don't act superior just because you're talented."

Several heads cocked to see Dwight's reaction to that one, but his scornful expression didn't shift.

"Acknowledge everyone's importance and contribution to the organization.

"Listen to others and ensure we fully understand their positions."

Guy thanked Andy and asked if anyone wanted to suggest any changes. No one said anything. In fact, a good portion of them were staring at the greenish-gray carpet. Guy turned to Dwight, wishing he could just ignore the man. "You have the floor," he said.

"That list reads like a to-do list for wasting time," Dwight began without hesitation. "I can't...I *won't* be held to those standards. Trying to find something nice to say to everyone and pretending everyone is of equal importance...." Dwight trailed off, spreading his hands to emphasize the level of his exasperation.

"Andy, could you re-read the list...," Guy began, but Dwight kept going.

"...I mean, is this a workplace or Willy Wonka's Chocolate Factory? We are busy. This is a huge project we're looking at. Maybe because I have more experience than a lot of people here,

I know how hard it's going to be to get it done and to get it right."

The room was dead quiet.

Even Guy didn't speak until he was sure Dwight was finished. "So what I hear you saying is that this list makes you feel like you won't be able to do your job if you have to adhere to all these behaviors. They're too time-consuming. Is that your objection?"

"Yes, that's what I'm saying. They're unrealistic, too. Frankly, the people who are going to run around having fun enforcing them probably don't have enough real work to do." Dwight folded his arms and looked straight at Guy, clearly challenging his boss's judgment.

"In your opinion," Guy added.

"In my opinion," Dwight confirmed, his tone the very essence of arrogance.

At the moment, Guy wished that he could hand off his responsibilities as leader to someone else. He didn't much care who that someone else was, as long as he didn't have to handle Dwight anymore. But he had to press on and make his point.

"Okay, good," said Guy, shoving his left hand in his pocket and trying to appear relaxed. "What's important, Dwight, is that I understand what you're saying before I jump to any misguided conclusions. Isn't that right?"

"Yes."

"And how did it feel to you when I checked first about what you said, instead of going ahead and reacting to what I might have *thought* you said?"

"It felt very good."

Guy knew that Dwight could tell where he was going with this line of questioning, but at least Dwight respected his boss's authority enough to give honest answers in front of the group. Guy breathed a mental sigh of relief for that small mercy.

"Now, that took a little bit of time," Guy concluded. "But what if we had just started talking past each other? Do you think we would have taken up even more time?"

"Probably."

"Okay, so that's one instance, and just one instance, in which taking the time to understand you fully might have ended up saving time. Will you grant me that?"

"Okay." It was a terse answer, but it was enough. Guy had made his point, and he had—he hoped—retained the respect of his employees.

"Okay. Let's take a break." Everyone certainly needed one.

CHAPTER 11

A Temporary Truce

Dwight was quiet and withdrawn for the rest of the day's exercises. He fiddled with his BlackBerry from time to time, even though the room had voted against checking text messages. But no one called Dwight on it. Guy decided to ignore it, too. He recalled a saying from childhood: "Let the baby have his bottle." There was wisdom in that after all these years.

When the day was finally over and everyone had started to pack up, Guy called Dwight into his office and closed the door.

"Well, that was a pretty negative scene there for a while earlier today," Guy began, motioning for Dwight to take a seat. "I'm curious what you made of it."

"What I made of it?" Dwight asked, blinking. He'd entered the room bracing himself to be lectured, and it seemed that all Guy wanted was his opinion.

"Yeah, what did you make of it?" Guy repeated. "Do you think it helped us—me, you, the company?"

"It was probably valuable for some of the younger people here," Dwight acknowledged. He was cautious, as though he was waiting for Guy to spring a trap. "And it was probably good for you, to see the whole company marching along to Argosy's tune."

Guy was silent for a moment, thinking. Then he steepled his fingers and leaned forward.

"You know, Dwight," he said, "people on your team have complained to me about your attitude in the past. I always urged them to kind of suck it up. I mean, if I had to deal with J.W. and his foolishness, why shouldn't some kid out of college have to deal with Dwight Jones, right?"

Dwight smiled, the skin around his eyes crinkling.

"Yeah, I thought it was kind of funny until today," Guy went on. "But I've been listening all day to the people who work around you, and I have to say, I really heard them for the first time."

Guy drew a deep breath.

"So I need your advice. What can we do about this?"

Dwight stared at his boss, his eyebrows drawing together. He looked a little shaken.

"Is that what that whole values thing is about?" he asked. "Is it some kind of witch hunt for dissenters?"

"No, it is not," Guy replied in a firm tone. "I am sincerely asking you if there is any way I can help you improve your attitude toward your co-workers in this company, because, without pointing a finger of blame, what's happening now is not working."

"Look, if this is about my lack of enthusiasm for the whole rah-rah team stuff, well, I'm not a football player," Dwight's tone grew defensive, and he began to unconsciously jiggle his foot against Guy's desk. "I'm not a jock, and I don't go for that stuff."

"Dwight, I know that there are people who look at this face of mine and think to themselves, *big dumb jock*," Guy acknowledged. He smiled, although there was little humor in it. "But you know me better than that. You know I'm more than a college football player. I'm a graphic designer, just like you. I'm not as good at it as you are, but I know what it takes. You need a sharp, critical mind. You need creative focus. And I know it helps the finished product that you have a low tolerance for mediocrity and imperfection."

Guy drew another deep breath. "But I also know that when I work in close proximity with other people, I can't judge them the way I would judge a poorly executed web page. Even if I feel like it."

"It's not my fault," Dwight said. He crossed his arms belligerently. Clearly, he wasn't going to make this easy. "It's the way I am. That's how I contribute. Let other people around here be all sunshine and light while I crank out the goods and win us some awards. Isn't that enough teamwork for you?"

Guy shook his head. "No, it's not. You're the leader of a team made up of younger people who respect you and your talent, and who desperately hope that you will return the courtesy. They look up to you and would like to follow your example, but they sometimes don't see that much to admire."

Dwight's face registered shock. "They said that?"

"Not to me. But they've said it."

Dwight looked away and pursed his lips. Guy almost expected him to begin rolling his eyes. "I never asked to be anyone's role model."

"I understand," Guy said, drawing yet another long breath to ensure that he didn't say anything in haste that he would regret later. "But that is the responsibility you have here. So let me ask you this: Do you think you would be happier without that responsibility, somewhere else?"

"You're not firing me, are you?" This time, Dwight truly did look as though the rug had been pulled out from underneath him. His fists were clenched on the arms of his chair.

"I'm trying to light a fire *under* you," Guy said, inclining his head to emphasize his point. He tried to sound empathic but not pleading. "I can't have a debate with you about why respect or integrity matters. You know why? Because this whole workplace just spent a day finishing that debate. They all agreed to some very clear and observable behaviors that express what are now Eaton/Argosy's core values. And these are now the normative behaviors expected of everyone in this building, by the consensus of everyone in this building.

"So if anyone—including myself—behaves otherwise and violates these core values, there's no more room for interpretation," he continued. "We all, as a team, have determined what is and isn't acceptable here, starting today. When it comes to these behaviors, it's now going to be very obvious to the whole team whenever one horse pulls in the wrong direction. Do you understand?"

Dwight blinked. He looked down at his shoes and then stood up. "Communication clear. Good night."

He shook Guy's hand and walked out.

Just a few years ago, a confrontation like this would have given Guy the shakes—before, during, and after. But now, Guy felt strangely calm and focused. An entire day of discussions over values and behaviors had given him a sense of clarity he'd never felt before. Leadership was indeed a choice. Now Dwight Jones, with all his design awards to commend him, was free to choose or reject Guy's leadership. Guy felt like the decision was out of his hands.

Then he remembered Ellen's web portfolio on Dwight's computer screen. He needed to make sure his expectations on that front were clear as well. Before leaving for home, he wrote an email memo to the staff:

Thank you all for a great first Values Day at Eaton/Argosy. I am so excited to be working with such a first-rate group of people, and I know that TrekPhone is going to be a first-rate campaign as a result of the work we did today!

There's a little issue I'd like to clear up that involves behavior related to the core value of "Integrity." You are all smart, creative people, and I am personally committed to your professional development. That may mean that some of you do occasional work outside the office for other people. That's fine with me, as long as those people aren't our competitors.

However, your hours while you're here—and the use of Eaton/Argosy equipment—should be limited to the work you're doing for Eaton/Argosy. There can be occasional, reasonable exceptions to the rule, of course, but only if you notify your immediate supervisor, and if your supervisor notifies me.

Integrity is the one value that underlies all the others. Let's not treat it casually.

There, Guy thought as he clicked "send." *Now we'll see if the communication really* was *clear, as Dwight claimed—and whether his handshake was a sincere sign of agreement or a devious precursor to mutiny.*

Chapter 12

A Briefcase, a Brandover... and a Bully Report

It had taken almost a month with two cancellations in between, but Guy had finally landed a lunch appointment with Arnie Mann, Argosy's creative director.

The two men took a sidewalk table at a restaurant on Rittenhouse Square, and before long Arnie was regaling Guy with Ted Stone stories. Arnie, a doughy man with a thick head of prematurely gray hair, didn't seem to mind if the diners at adjacent tables heard what he was saying.

"Has anyone told you the 'Briefcase in Vegas' story?" Arnie asked Guy, taking a bite of his yeast roll. "No? Oh, this is great. It's pure Ted. We're out in Vegas for a trade show, and you need to know that Ted has this thing for very expensive briefcases by Crouch and Fitzgerald. Now, the way I see it, the problem with having an expensive briefcase is that it's a thief magnet. A thief won't even care what's in it, because the briefcase itself is worth stealing."

Guy raised his eyebrows. "Someone stole Ted's briefcase in Las Vegas?"

Arnie nodded vigorously, wiping bread crumbs off of his chin. "It was filled with all this stuff we needed for a late afternoon meeting. When we flew in to the Vegas airport, we sent all our baggage ahead to the hotel. Then we went straight to the blackjack tables, because Ted loves blackjack. Anyway, once we're done and Ted is up a few thousand from the tables, we take a cab to the hotel. Everything is waiting for us at the hotel, except for that Crouch and Fitzgerald briefcase."

"Oh, no." Shading his eyes against the sun, Guy kept his gaze trained on Arnie.

"Oh, yes. It's gone. I'm about to go nuts!"

Arnie was gesticulating so expansively that Guy was afraid he'd knock his drink off the table. "I'm ready to run to the desk and demand they call the cops. But Ted is calm. He's just looking around, scanning the lobby, and he says to me, 'I'll stay here, Arnie. You go find the head bellman.' So I go and get the bellman, and I'm trying not to say too much to the guy. I just tell him that we've got a big problem and that he needs to come and see my boss right away."

"You didn't tell him about the briefcase."

Arnie shook his head. "Once you know that Ted Stone has a plan, you learn to say very little. I could tell from the way Ted asked me to find the bellman that he had something up his sleeve. So I bring the bellman, and Ted reaches into his pocket and takes out two $100 chips from the Bellagio. And he puts his hand on the bellman's shoulder, and says, 'I'm missing a valuable dark brown Crouch and Fitzgerald briefcase. There are papers in it that we need for a meeting at four. Here, take these.' And he gives the bellman the chips. Then he says, 'We'll be waiting in the bar.'"

"He didn't say anything else?"

"He said so little that it scared the heck out of that bellman. Ten minutes later, the man comes into the bar with the brief-case. He apologizes for the 'mix-up' and even tries to give Ted his chips back."

Guy had to admit that he was intrigued. "Ted knew the bell-man had his briefcase?" he asked.

"Here's what Ted told me," Arnie said, leaning forward as though he was about to impart a carefully guarded secret. "He was certain only a professional thief would know to take a Crouch and Fitzgerald briefcase. And he knew that a thief can't work a hotel lobby unless he pays off the head bellman. So all Ted had to do was hint to the bellman that he knew the score, and the bellman folded. He and the thief got cold feet, and they gave back the briefcase as fast as they could."

"But why would he give the bellman a tip for stealing?" Guy picked up the last bite of his club sandwich and chewed on it while he listened to Arnie's enthusiastic answer.

"The chips from the Bellagio? The chips were a master-stroke. The chips told the bellman, 'I am someone for whom $200 is pocket change. I'm not mad now, but imagine what I am capable of if I give you $200 and you don't bring me my brief-case.' Brilliant."

Guy had to admit that Ted wasn't a man to be trifled with. "So did you call the cops or tell the manager?"

"What? Get the bellman arrested so we'd have to fly back a month later to testify?" Arnie shook his head in a patronizing manner. "Be serious! We had to prepare for our meeting. And so what if the bellman was a crook? Vegas is full of crooks. That's not exactly our problem."

Guy's sense of right and wrong was offended. "Yeah, but there was a theft ring operating in that hotel."

"You're missing the point of the story. Ted Stone knew exactly what he needed to do to get the result he wanted. He has a gift for knowing these things. That's why this is my favorite Ted Stone story. You'll hear others, but this one is my absolute favorite."

Guy wondered if Arnie truly held Ted Stone in as high esteem as his story suggested. To hear Arnie tell it, Ted could do no wrong, and Arnie was a bit old for hero worship.

Arnie took a bite of food, and changed the subject. "So, how are you all doing with the TrekPhone recycling thing?"

Guy blinked. "Recycling thing?"

"Linda didn't tell you?" Arnie swirled his fork around his plate, attempting to capture the last remnants of his fettuccine alfredo.

"Maybe she did and I forgot," Guy was trying to recover. He was glad that the other man was looking down at his plate and not across the table at him. He had never heard the word "recycling" associated with the TrekPhone, and he was pretty sure his face showed it.

"Oh, you wouldn't have forgotten this," Arnie began, looking up. "The whole TrekPhone campaign has to be done over—at least your piece of it. We sent a bunch of new materials over to Linda last week from CellMobile. They did some deeper market research and discovered two things. One, children and young people under 30 are the ideal market for the TrekPhone. And two, children and young people under 30 *hate* the word 'disposable.' A disposable phone sounds wasteful, like you're helping kill the planet when you throw one away. So even though these two groups are the ideal market for the TrekPhone, most of them don't want anything to do with it."

Guy tried to hide his rising sense of panic. He forced himself to take a deep breath. Why hadn't Linda told him about this?

"Now here's the twist," Arnie continued, thankfully oblivious to Guy's distress. "If we tell those same children and young adults that the TrekPhone is 'recyclable' instead of 'disposable,' then they love the phone! So now CellMobile wants a new 'green' marketing plan that includes a nationwide network of drop-off points for recycling TrekPhones. All the new designs have got to emphasize recycling. And polar bears. They want a tie-in for saving the polar bears from the melting Arctic icecap."

Guy latched on to an idea he could wrap his brain around. "What will CellMobile do with all the broken phones they collect?"

"I have no idea," Arnie replied. "I don't even know for a fact that CellMobile intends to recycle them. What I do know is that they want to *say* they're recycling TrekPhones in big screaming typefaces. Their numbers on this are pretty clear. CellMobile has got tens of millions invested in the TrekPhone, but if we launch the marketing campaign the way it looks this minute, the Trek-Phone will be DOA. It will go down in history like New Coke or the Edsel."

Guy needed a moment to collect his thoughts, so he excused himself to go to the men's room. He called Linda from the adjacent vestibule. "What is Arnie telling me? TrekPhone with a recycling theme?"

"We just got the materials today," Linda said. Her voice sounded strained. "We have to start all over. With everything."

"Today? Arnie said he sent them over last week!" Guy pinched the bridge of his nose with his free hand.

"That's cute," Linda said. Her tone had a dangerous edge to it now. "The stuff I got is backdated all over. The Argosy ad people are pretending they sent this to us last week because they don't want the delay to be on their heads. They think it will be easy to blame the new kids for being late."

"And they're right," Guy replied. He rubbed his eyes. How had a lunch he'd anticipated for so long gone south so quickly? "Arnie Mann is tight with Ted. When I get back I'll tell you a story about Arnie and Ted's briefcase. Arnie knows I can't go running to Ted and complaining that we need more time."

"That's fine," said Linda, "but you're going to have to talk to Dwight yourself about this. I can't tell him that everything he's done for the past two weeks needs to be junked just because CellMobile finally decided to do some real consumer research."

"Linda," Guy heaved a sigh. He couldn't seem to think straight. "What do you think I need to do about Dwight?"

"There's nothing you *can* do," she said. "He great and he's impossible. He's probably impossible because he knows he's great. Don't worry about him so much. No one at the office expects you to do anything about him anyway."

"They don't?"

"No. They all know we need him, and they understand why you can't risk losing him. People either adapt to Dwight or they leave." Guy could almost hear Linda's shrug over the phone. "You've noticed the turnover in Dwight's corner of the office, haven't you?"

Guy's brow furrowed. "Yeah, but isn't that just about young programmers and designers switching jobs, coming and going?"

"It's partly that," Linda admitted. "But it's mostly about Dwight. The older people in the office feel pretty resigned that Dwight's here to stay, but the younger people, they're more mobile. They just flee. Do you have time to hear what I overheard in the women's room?"

"The women's room?" Guy asked, intrigued. "Always."

"One of our twentysomethings said to another that once you get on Dwight's bad side, you first get your resume together, and then you get out. There's no point in complaining because Mr. Big Guy won't do anything."

A nickname. That stung. "*I'm* Mr. Big Guy?"

"It's not the worst nickname I've ever heard."

Guy was indignant. "I'd rather be called Wally!"

"This is why that new designer Margie left so quickly a few months ago. Dwight chased her off."

"I never got to talk to her," Guy said, leaning back against the vestibule wall. "She skipped her exit interview."

"Okay, now we're into rumors, and I don't like to bother you with rumors. But the story goes that Dwight threatened to ruin her reputation if she complained to you. I don't know how much stock to put into that. And even if it's true, what can you do about it? I mean, realistically."

There was a tone in Linda's voice that Guy never thought he'd hear. He had caught a whiff of the problem on Values Day, and now he saw confirming evidence everywhere. He was losing the staff's respect. They were pulling away from him. Even Linda was giving up.

The office bully was running everyone down, and Mr. Big Guy was doing nothing to protect them.

CHAPTER 13

Turning on a Dime

When Guy returned from lunch with Arnie Mann, he went straight to Dwight with the bad news that the disposable phone campaign was, itself, disposable.

"I knew it," Dwight grumbled when Guy finished explaining. "What did I tell you about these people? That first round of tweaks and changes they ordered was all a big waste of time, because now it's all garbage anyway."

"It's not Argosy, Dwight," Guy said, although privately he was less than pleased with Argosy himself. "The client had a big change in direction. And the research bears it out. This phone would be dead if we tried to sell it the way we planned."

"Argosy's not handling the client right," Dwight shot back. "They're giving us work before the client company knows what it wants. You know why? Because they know they can always tell us to do it over. And over. And over. How much time do we have to fix this?"

There was no use in lying, so Guy gave it to Dwight straight. "Ted Stone thinks we've had this recycling revamp on our desks for a week now. So we need to see something...."

"Yesterday," Dwight filled in, slamming his hand on the desk. "Yesterday would have been good. Is that what you're saying?"

Guy didn't disagree, because he knew Dwight was right. "Look, it's Friday afternoon. If there's anything you can pull together just to get them something to look at...."

"Argosy *weasels!*" Dwight hissed the words through his teeth as he started going through the research recommendations that Guy had given him. "Let me take a look at this."

The marketing strategy for TrekPhone had always called for putting Dwight's website design at the center of the campaign. It ensured that all other materials related to the campaign would benefit from Dwight's thematic approach. Now that the entire campaign had to be re-conceived around recycling, all other design work in the office ground to a halt. No one else could do any work until Dwight had a new web design completed and approved.

To Guy, it looked like this: Dwight was now at the head of a huge bottleneck in the workflow of the entire office. It was completely up to Dwight when the bottleneck would clear. There was nothing Guy could do about it, a reality that made his stomach churn.

"What's this?" Dwight asked, still reviewing the new information from CellMobile. "It says we need a 'web-integrated' process for sending back damaged phones?" He paused. "Okay. Okay. I'm on it."

Dwight's face took on a faraway look. He was mentally locking in. He stood up and poked his head over the wall of his cubicle, addressing the young designer to his left. "Hey, we're going to need some new sub-pages for this re-design. Stop what you're doing. Stop. Right. Now."

Dwight was rude but efficient. He was in control. He was what Guy needed right now. Guy didn't remind Dwight about the importance of treating people with respect. Instead, he stepped away without a word.

CHAPTER 14

The Dwight Vise Tightens

"It's a shame you can't just shut him off in his own room and email him instructions," Melanie was saying to Guy. The children were asleep, and the couple was talking quietly in the living room. "Dwight would probably like that, wouldn't he?"

"He might," Guy replied. Guy himself would like it even more, he didn't bother adding. "But our web designs need too much collaboration for that. And Dwight knows he needs other people to pick up all the scutwork that he feels is beneath him. He's just rude and dismissive to most of them. And the situation may be worse than I even know. I'm beginning to wish J.W. had never hired him."

"Hey, how *is* J.W. doing at Argosy?" Melanie swung her feet up onto the throw pillow on Guy's lap.

"J.W.?" Guy asked, folding his hands on top of his wife's feet. "Gone."

"Gone?" Melanie's right eyebrow rose until it almost disappeared under her sideswept bangs. It was a trademark expression of hers.

Guy nodded. "He never had a chance. Once J.W. took Ted and Arnie around to meet with the four or five major accounts we had, Argosy was done with him. He was smart, though. He made them buy him out. It was all in the terms of the merger."

"So what's he doing now?"

"Golfing. Fishing. I don't know." Whatever he was up to, J.W. sure wasn't dealing with the mess Guy had on his plate.

Melanie opened her mouth as though she was about to say something, but Guy spoke first. "I gotta go talk to Stanley. My severance deal with Argosy isn't nearly as sweet as J.W.'s." He walked into the kitchen and picked up the phone.

"So your star performer isn't exactly living the values, huh?" Stanley said it like it was a familiar problem, which gave Guy a sense of relief.

"You've seen this kind of thing before?" Guy opened the fridge door and looked over the shelves in an absentminded manner.

"It happens all the time," Stanley replied. "Some people get special treatment their whole lives because of their talent. They start assuming the rules don't apply to them. The problem is that they are absolute poison. On a boat or in a workplace."

Guy nodded as he grabbed a soda with his free hand and kicked the refrigerator door closed. "Poison is the word. It's like he's got a toxic cloud around him. I keep trying to either detox him or contain the cloud. Nothing's worked."

"You have to start documenting each instance of insubordination," Stanley said. He was matter-of-fact. "That's the first step, if you haven't been doing it already."

"What, so I can fire him?" As much of a problem as Dwight was, Guy couldn't quite make the mental leap that imagining Eaton without him required. He popped his soda can open.

"Guy, did you or did you not agree with me that he's poison?" Obviously, Stanley's view of the situation included fewer shades of gray than Guy's did.

"Sure, but I don't know if I can do without him. He's our award-winning head of web design!"

"You've told me all about the great work he does. But what you're doing now is making excuses for him," Stanley chided.

"I've spoiled him," Guy said. He took a sip of his soda and wiped his mouth with the back of his hand. "I know."

"You're also avoiding something difficult and unpleasant." Stanley tried not to sound harsh. "It's perfectly natural. But it's not leadership. Have you taken stock of how his behavior is affecting your ability to lead?"

Guy hesitated, giving the question serious thought. "Linda told me a few things the other day. The younger people say I'll never do anything about Dwight. They even have a nickname for me now."

"I remember Linda," Stanley said. "She's a smart woman. You're lucky to have her on your side. So listen to her. She's trying to tell you something. As I recall, the hot buttons in your personal leadership philosophy include gossip and nicknames. Your younger people are pressing those buttons and they don't even care if Linda knows it."

"That's bad, isn't it?" Guy knew that it was.

"What's worse is that I get the feeling you don't even know the people who work around Dwight because so many leave so fast. You might want to call a few who quit recently. Find out more about the circumstances, now that they've got no reason to cover for him. Once you hear those details, maybe you'll have an easier time coming to a decision."

By the time Guy got off the phone with Stanley, Melanie was getting ready for bed herself. Guy slumped on the couch and flicked on *SportsCenter*. Athletic scores were a lot easier to understand than his current predicament.

"Hey," Melanie said, poking her head into the den. She bit her upper lip. "We need to talk about that health reimbursement account. There's something I need to say."

Guy turned off the television, sensing that he was in the doghouse. "I told you it was my fault and that I'm sorry. What else can I do?"

"I still feel terrible about it," Melanie replied, coming over to sit next to him.

"Don't. Maybe when we talk to our accountant, he can figure out a way to itemize our medical expenses and get some of that money back." Guy tried to reassure his wife, but Melanie became visibly upset, twisting the fringe on one of the throw pillows.

"It's not just the money," she said. Her voice began to quiver. "I was so proud that I had thought of this. I used to be a pretty sharp accountant. But I've been home for almost eight years now, first with Donna, and then with Molly. I haven't had a chance to contribute financially to this household in a long time."

Guy put his arm around his wife and pulled her head onto his shoulder. "It was a good idea, Honey."

However, Melanie wouldn't be placated that easily. She sat back up. "I know it was, and that's what makes me so sad." She began to tear up. "All this drama at work over Dwight these past few weeks has consumed you. It seems like it's all you talk about, or think about. And this little thing that was so important to me, you just looked at it like it was nothing, like my contribution was meaningless. You never thought it might mean something to me, beyond the money, did you?"

"No," Guy admitted. "I didn't." He hadn't felt like this big of a scumbag in a long time.

"I researched the information, got the forms from the orthodontist, got the government forms, and prepared everything for you. So when you forgot about the paperwork in your briefcase, I felt like you'd forgotten about me. I felt so insignificant. Then you acted like a thousand dollars was nothing we'd miss. It made me feel like I was nothing you'd miss, either."

There was nothing for Guy to say. He held Melanie in his arms as she sobbed. He told himself they should get a sitter and do something special together that weekend, so he could try to make up for his thoughtlessness. But for the rest of the weekend, Guy thought of little else but Dwight Jones.

CHAPTER 15

Rewards and Revelations

Monday morning brought a message from Ted Stone on Guy's BlackBerry.

G-

Love the recycling website. Good work!

Ted

Guy checked his email. Over the weekend, Dwight had re-done the TrekPhone website with a bright green and yellow recycling theme. There were lots of blank spaces indicating a need for more text, but the tone and approach was sound. There were polar bears, too. Dwight had turned it around in record time, without a deadline.

But Dwight had also pulled a fast one in the way he handled the finished product. He should have sent the website links around to the other department heads first for comment, and then on to Guy for final approval. Instead, Dwight had emailed the links to everyone in the office. He had also emailed them to Ted Stone and Arnie Mann. Clearly, he wanted everyone to know that this was his work, and his work alone.

That made it a little easier to do what Guy needed to do next. "Sonia," he asked his assistant, "can you get me phone numbers for the last three web designers who left us?"

"Will do," she replied, and closed Guy's office door behind her.

The first number Sonia retrieved was for Margie Kranitz, the young woman who had skipped her exit interview with Guy when she quit two months earlier. Guy had a vague memory of her—she'd been quiet, but a head of thick auburn hair had made her stand out.

As it turned out, Margie was now at a small web design shop, just a few blocks away. Guy dialed the shop's number and asked for her. There was a long wait before she picked up, during which time Guy scrolled through the weekend's accumulation of emails.

"Margie, this is Guy Cedrick at the Eaton Group," he introduced himself. "How are you?"

"I'm fine," Margie said. Her tone was clipped. "Why are you calling me?"

Guy hadn't expected Margie to be quite so direct. He wanted to feel her out a bit more before getting to the real point of his call.

"You know, we're part of Argosy now, and since you and I never got a chance to talk after you left, I wanted to check in," he improvised. "I wanted to see if you'd ever consider coming back."

"Are you hiring?" Margie sounded a bit confused, and Guy couldn't blame her.

"We may be hiring soon, and we like to keep a list of designers on hand who might be interested in working here," he said. "A lot has changed now that we're with Argosy."

"Is Dwight Jones still there?"

The blunt question took Guy by surprise, causing him to stop sorting through his email and give his full attention to Margie. Apparently, he wouldn't have to steer the conversation around to the real purpose of his call, after all.

"Yes, he is. He said some nice things about your work, and that's partly why I'm calling."

Margie chuckled, but to Guy it didn't sound like she was amused. "No, he didn't."

"Excuse me?"

"Why would he say nice things about my work? All he did was criticize me when I was there. He was mean and personal about it, too."

"I didn't know that," Guy replied, and then added silently, *but I'm not surprised.* He had expected to get this type of response before he had ever dialed Margie's number.

"No, I guess you didn't," Margie told him. "I contacted a lawyer about Dwight Jones, okay? When I confronted Dwight about how he talked to me, he told me that if I complained to you or Linda he'd make sure I never worked in town again. Then he started bragging about all the people he knows in web design in Philly."

A lawyer? This *was* a surprise to Guy. He ran a hand through his short hair. "Margie," he said, "I owe you an apology. That should never happen to anyone here. And I want to take some steps to make sure it never happens to anyone again."

The line was silent for a second. "Just don't tell Dwight you talked to me, okay?" Margie said it in a pleading voice. Even now, Dwight Jones made her nervous. "I don't want anything to do with him, and I don't want him to think I'm complaining about him. I'd like to forget I ever worked there, okay?"

At that moment, a flurry of movement caught Guy's eye from between the half-open blinds on his floor-to-ceiling office window, so he got up and opened his door a crack. There was a sudden commotion around Dwight's corner of the office, and a crowd was forming around his desk. Dwight signed a slip from a bicycle messenger and started opening a small box.

Guy put one hand over the phone receiver. "Sonia," he said, looking around the doorframe, "could you see what that's about?"

He returned to his call. "Margie, I understand how you must feel. You'll have no problems from Dwight. I'm just calling some former employees to see if there's anything we could have done to keep them with us."

"So now you know the answer, don't you?"

Sonia slid a note onto Guy's desk. It read:

Ted Stone just sent Dwight a gift certificate for dinner for four at Le Bec-Fin.

"Yes I do, Margie." Guy's tone was grim. "I've got to go now. Thank you very much."

Le Bec-Fin was the best French restaurant in Philadelphia. Guy had been there exactly twice, and he knew the math. Dinner for four with wine was worth at least $700. It looked like Ted Stone had a new pet employee.

Later that morning, Arnie Mann called.

"Hey, I wanted to deliver some news," Arnie said. "You got Ted's note about the TrekPhone redesign?"

"He loves it," Guy replied. "I know. He just sent over a Le Bec-Fin gift certificate for Dwight Jones."

"Oh, that's not because Ted loves the site," Arnie informed him. "You need to know this. Ted doesn't send around dinners just because he likes something. Dinners are for results."

Guy frowned. "I don't get it," he told the other man. "What results? The website isn't even live yet."

"This is why I'm calling!" Guy could tell that Arnie was starting to get excited. His voice was getting louder and louder. "Ted liked the redesign enough to send it around to some friends at agencies that represent big retailers. He's been telling CellMobile all along that that's the direction they should go, with big retail. So here's the news. He got a nibble from MegaMart's ad agency."

"MegaMart?" Guy was genuinely shocked. MegaMart was the world's largest retailer.

"We're talking big, big money potential here. MegaMart's ad agency liked the site, liked the design, and they love the way the recycling program works. So much so that they want to try incorporating it into the MegaMart Online shopping site, as though it were a page on the MegaMart site." Arnie delivered this last bit of news in reverent tones.

"Has MegaMart ever done that before?" The concept didn't sound familiar to Guy.

"What? Put another company's product page on their website? No. Never. They had been talking about it, but this was the first time they felt they had a product, a partner, and a design that might work for them. So they might be willing to give it a try. Just talking to MegaMart's agency is a huge step. And that's why Dwight got those dinners at Le Bec-Fin," Arnie explained.

"How many visitors does the MegaMart Online store get every day?"

"It ranks something like fourth or fifth after Amazon and a few others. It's huge. Anyway, they need to work out the technical details and give your design team the specs for MegaMart Online. Should I just give them Dwight's number?"

"Yeah," said Guy. He was stunned. "But give them my numbers, too. Including my cell phone, in case there are any problems."

"Problems?" Arnie inquired. Clearly, he was still on Cloud Nine.

"Dwight's an artist." Guy let Arnie use his imagination about his meaning. He remembered the briefcase story. The less said with these people, the better.

Arnie paused. "Got it."

As he hung up the phone, Guy wished he could say the same.

CHAPTER 16

Values Upheld

The TrekPhone marketing campaign took shape in the following weeks. Everyone on the Eaton/Argosy team threw themselves into figuring out new "green" aspects of the product that they hadn't considered before. The TrekPhone was booked for appearances at environmental trade shows. Contacts were made with networks of pro-environment retail shops and cable news shows. Press contacts, websites, and bloggers were kept up to date about the pending autumn launch.

The web tie-in with MegaMart Online, on the other hand, was more difficult than anyone could have guessed. One technical glitch after another prevented Dwight's TrekPhone page from working as a part of MegaMart Online. Dwight was getting exasperated trying to figure out the problems with MegaMart and its ad agency.

"These people are so arrogant!" he complained one day to Guy after slamming his phone down into its cradle. If he'd been a cartoon, steam would have been whistling out of his ears. "They want me to change our page design to accommodate their site specs, but their website is a total *kludgebucket*." The word was programmer slang for anything jerry-rigged and slapped together.

"Don't tell them their site is a kludgebucket, whatever you do," Guy told him. He didn't completely trust the other man *not* to do it. "This is going to take patience, Dwight. MegaMart is the proverbial 500-pound gorilla, and they've got to be treated that way."

Dwight just looked him. He didn't get the reference. Guy plastered a smile onto his face. "You know where a 500-pound gorilla sleeps, don't you?" he asked.

"In the jungle?" Dwight's expression was put-upon.

"A 500-pound gorilla sleeps anywhere he wants!"

"I hate jokes like that." Dwight scowled and looked back at this computer screen.

Guy's false smile quickly fell off his face. "Yeah, but they've got a grain of truth in them, Dwight. We've got to do whatever these people want, because they are MegaMart and we're...." Guy waved his hand through the air, searching for a word that wouldn't completely belittle Eaton/Argosy.

"We're not." Dwight nodded. "Look, whatever happened to all the cool little start-up clients we used to have?"

"I think you remember," Guy told him. "The coolest ones worked us to death, didn't pay us, and then went broke."

Dwight laughed and went back to his desk.

For the next few days, Guy didn't hear about MegaMart. He assumed the technical fixes were working out. Then one day a young web designer named Mike showed up at Guy's door. He looked terrified.

"Uh, Dwight's not here, but I thought I should tell you," he stammered. "The guy from MegaMart just hung up on me."

Guy looked up from the printout he'd been examining. "He what?"

"He hung up on me. He was insisting I make changes that I knew Dwight wouldn't do, and when I tried to explain it, he just said something like, 'I've had it with you people,' and he hung up."

Guy paused to take this in, sitting back in his chair. "Okay, my first question, Mike—and this is no knock on you—but why are you on the phone with MegaMart?"

Mike shuffled a few steps further into Guy's office. "Two days ago, Dwight announced to us that he couldn't deal with them anymore," he explained. "He told me to start screening his calls from them. So I began talking to the MegaMart folks, and soon, I was kind of the go-between. It was working for a while, but these last things they wanted, I mean, I tried to warn them."

Guy sighed, suddenly feeling exhausted. "Mike, no one on earth warns MegaMart of anything."

Mike shook his head. "Dwight does. I've heard him do it."

Guy didn't doubt it. And he hoped that he'd be able to undo some of the damage that Dwight's inflexibility had caused. "Do me a favor, Mike. Go see Linda right away and tell her your story. Tell her that I'm calling Arnie Mann. And thank you, Mike, for coming to me with this."

"Amy Mann?" Mike was drawing a blank.

"Arnie. Tell Linda I'm calling Arnie Mann."

This looked bad. Usually two businesses wouldn't let a spitting match between web designers blow up a deal, but this was MegaMart. The company was famous for having no tolerance for rocky partnerships. You do it MegaMart's way, or they find another partner. Guy needed Arnie's advice.

"Don't panic," Arnie told Guy after he had explained the situation. "I'll call our friend at the agency and we'll try to dial it back. Who was this kid on the phone with MegaMart?"

"His name is Mike."

"Why would you let some kid...?" Arnie cut himself off. "Never mind, Guy. I'm glad you called. We'll try and get the toothpaste back in the tube right away."

Guy looked out into the main section of the office. Dwight had returned from wherever he'd been and was sitting back at his desk. He had a sour expression on his face. Nothing new there. But Guy knew that it was time for his own behavior to take another, much tougher direction.

Guy buzzed Dwight and asked him to come in and close the door.

"Mike just had a fight with someone at MegaMart," he began without preamble.

Dwight shrugged. "I told you those people were jerks. Absolute jerks."

"And *I* told *you* we've got to do whatever they want. What part of that didn't you get?" Guy was seething, but he kept his tone even.

"I was handling it!" Dwight was instantly defensive. "I know my limits. When I couldn't take it anymore, I asked Mike to start taking their calls. He's a very pleasant, capable person. Everyone likes Mike. I thought things would go smoother with MegaMart if he took their calls."

The explanation was logical on the surface, but Guy doubted that Dwight had put forth any effort at all to work amicably with the MegaMart designers.

"Why didn't you come to me?" Guy asked. He could at least give Dwight the opportunity to explain himself.

"I was trying to handle it myself, in my own way," Dwight explained. "What would *you* have done? Would you have taken their calls?"

Guy glanced out the window, steeling himself, then back into Dwight's eyes. This was it. "Dwight, this is the wrong job for you, isn't it?"

"Oh, no. Here we go."

Dwight actually rolled his eyes, and for the first time Guy completely understood how untouchable the man thought he was.

"I have tried to impress upon you the importance of understanding what values mean in this place, and here's a practical example staring us in the face. What do we do when we can't meet a commitment with a customer? We go to our supervisor. That's what I just did. I called Arnie Mann. That's what Mike *tried* to do. Everyone here seems to know this but you."

Dwight let his breath out in a short burst. "I was doing what I thought was best."

"By your own estimation," Guy clarified, holding up a finger. "Not by our values. Not by our agreed-upon behaviors. And that's why I'm asking for your resignation today."

Dwight's eyes widened, and for a moment no sound came out of his mouth. "You're firing me?"

Guy pressed his lips together. "I would like to give you the opportunity to resign so you can tell your friends you want to devote all your energies to DJDesign—yes, I saw your business cards. You're a brilliant designer, but we need a webmaster here who can work with young people, mentor them, train them, and do it the way we all do it here, with our values, our behaviors, and our procedures. Otherwise, we end up with messes, like today's mess with MegaMart."

Dwight started to get angry. "You're going to be sorry, Guy," he said with a sneer. "Have you cleared this with Ted?"

"Don't be like that, Dwight. I've been calling the young web designers who have quit on us over the past four months. What they've told me is cause enough for firing you without severance. So let's work this out like adults, okay?"

"Okay," Dwight said, deflating. For a moment he seemed defeated, but then he rallied. "You're all going to miss me a lot more than I'm going to miss this place."

"I'm sure that's true, Dwight." Guy told him. "That's the risk I have to take."

Guy had prepared the separation paperwork weeks ago and had it ready in his file drawer. Dwight signed a few forms and left without saying a word. Guy knew that he'd done the right thing, but he couldn't believe the last few minutes had actually happened. Unable to concentrate, he poured himself a glass of water and watched the activity outside his office.

Not long afterwards, Guy's BlackBerry buzzed.

It read:

G-

9 a.m.

T

The brevity. It sent a chill down Guy's spine.

On Walking Planks

Stanley Sabato was watering his lawn that evening when Guy pulled into the driveway next door.

"I fired Dwight today," Guy said, walking toward his neighbor.

Stanley looked up. "Today? Why today, of all days? I mean, what happened?"

"We had a problem, a big problem," Guy said. He shoved his keys into his pocket. "It was Dwight's fault and he had to go."

Stanley let out a low whistle, and moved his hose over to a row of potted flowers. "How did he take it?"

"Not as bad as I thought," Guy admitted. It was true—he wouldn't have been surprised if Dwight had resorted to physical violence. "He told me that I'd miss him more than he'd miss me."

"I doubt that," Stanley chuckled. "You should try this. Take a moment each day to stop and imagine what problem you're *not* dealing with at that instant because Dwight's gone. After a few days, you won't miss him at all."

Guy sighed, kicking at a rock with the toe of his loafer. "I don't know if I have a few days. Ted Stone might make me walk the plank tomorrow."

"Why? Just because you did what was needed? You defended the company's values, and now the whole staff knows it. Maybe you took too long to do it. He could fault you for that."

Guy wished it was that simple. "That's not going to be Ted's complaint," he replied. "He's upset about this big new problem. But he's going to be more upset that I fired Dwight."

Stanley frowned. "But Dwight caused the problem."

"Ted loves Dwight's work." Guy shrugged. *And he sure wasn't encouraging in his text message,* he thought but did not say.

"Look, when you go there tomorrow, keep in mind that Ted Stone is the one being tested," Stanley said, walking a few paces down his sidewalk to another cluster of plants. "You're testing him. And you might conclude it's time to make him and Argosy walk the plank."

Guy walked after his neighbor. "Stanley, what are you talking about?"

"You did your job," Stanley explained. "You did what was right for all your people. You upheld Argosy's core values and the behaviors that your staff spent a whole day attaching to those values. Now the question is, will Ted back you up?"

Guy didn't have to think about that one for very long. Again, that terse text message flashed in his mind.

"I'll be surprised if he does," Guy told Stanley. "He's a results-oriented boss, and my results are looking pretty poor today. MegaMart might quit on us, and I just fired the one person Ted was happy with. I feel like if I can't buy myself enough time to turn things around, I'm sunk."

"I won't argue with results," Stanley said. He turned the spigot until water spurted out of the hose in a few short bursts, then stopped. "Results are important. But when you put results above your core values, that's how you end up with Enron." Stanley started coiling up his garden hose. "If that's what Argosy is, another Enron, you'll know very soon. And you'll want no part of it."

Guy motioned with his hand, making an imaginary toast. "Wish me luck."

"You don't need luck," Stanley said with a half-smile. "You've got options, Guy. Don't waste your time with Argosy if this place can't live up to its own core values. If that's the case, and you stay with them too long, you're liable to catch whatever it is they've got."

"Thanks, Stanley," Guy said, recognizing the truth in the old sub captain's words. "That's exactly what I needed to hear right now."

Guy said this with a little more emotion than Stanley could handle. He changed the subject. "Walking the plank," Stanley said in a gruff voice, wiping the perspiration off his forehead. "It's mostly a myth, you know."

"What, pirates didn't make people walk the plank?"

Stanley grinned, and looked right at Guy. "Pirates couldn't be bothered with rigging up a plank. I guess you'd say they were very results-oriented. Once they were done with you, it was just a 'heave to' over the rail, and into the drink with the sharks!"

Great.

CHAPTER 18

Firing Fallout

When Guy entered Ted Stone's office the next morning, the older man had his back to the door and was facing his computer screen. Dwight's latest design of the TrekPhone website was opened to a page that invited retailers to log in and apply to carry the phone in their stores.

"Guy, have you gone over this page with Dwight?" Ted asked.

Guy murmured an assent. *Yikes,* he thought. *Does Ted not know?*

"Because it's got to be one of the best web-based sales interfaces I've seen." Dwight had developed the page with Guy's advice and the advice of a former Eaton Group salesperson whom Guy had brought in for consultation.

"I'd like to get you and Dwight up here to go over this page with our web design staff," Ted continued. "Maybe there's a way to adapt some of the best features here for our other clients' websites."

Guy nodded again and said nothing. Was this a joke? Was it some sort of test? Or was Ted just torturing him?

"But that's not why I asked you to come."

"I know." Guy's stomach was churning. He hadn't felt this nervous in years.

"Yeah, this MegaMart problem. I'm not very happy about it," Ted stated, swiveling his chair so that he was facing Guy. "Opportunities like this one don't come knocking very often, and it looks like we just slammed the door on opportunity's foot. Long-term, Guy, this could be a billion-dollar deal for TrekPhone. That's billion with a 'b.' And we're close to fumbling it."

Guy just listened, clenching his fists in his lap. He had resolved not to offer an explanation until Ted Stone asked him for one.

"Here's what I don't understand," Ted continued, bringing his hands down flat on the desk. "Why was someone named Mike down at your shop dealing with MegaMart's agency? I mean, how could you let that happen? They said Mike was obviously in over his head and then he got uncooperative."

Guy's jaw tightened. He focused his gaze on Ted's forehead. "I heard."

"Put yourself in the ad agency's shoes." Ted leaned back in his chair, clasping his hands behind his head in a relaxed pose that seemed to mock Guy's tenseness. "They put this deal together. They're representing the biggest retailer in the world, and they're risking their reputation by encouraging that retailer to partner with whom?"

He spread his hands, then continued in a tone of incredulity. "*With Mike from Philly?* Right now they want to drop this thing unless we can reassure them it can be fixed. My word is on the line. So tell me, what happened?"

Ted fixed Guy with an unwavering gaze.

"Dwight delegated that contact to Mike without consulting me." Guy said it very evenly. He had practiced this conversation on the way over. He would speak only in plain, observable facts. "That's what happened."

"So if you had known, you wouldn't have let Mike talk directly to MegaMart and the agency?"

"No, Mike's not ready for that." Guy said, shaking his head. "Dwight should have told me—no, check that, I should have *instructed* Dwight that if he experienced any difficulty with this, he should come to me immediately."

"Did you do that?" Ted cocked an eyebrow.

"No. No, I didn't."

"Why not?"

Guy was glad that he had a solid reason to explain his behavior. "Because everyone at Eaton/Argosy knows very well that when you can't keep a commitment on behalf of the company, you notify your supervisor. That's one of our integrity behaviors. It's also in my Personal Leadership Philosophy. That's why I called Arnie as soon as I learned about this."

Ted's eyebrows had drawn together. "You're talking in riddles, Guy. I'm asking you what happened."

"I'm sorry, Ted," Guy said, leaning his head back briefly. "I'm trying to take responsibility for this and not blame Dwight. The fact is, Dwight knew he needed to tell me he was having problems with MegaMart. He didn't want to come to me because he and I were already butting heads about other things. So he tried to bury the MegaMart problem by sticking it with Mike. But this is all ultimately my fault because Dwight should have been fired months ago."

"Fired?" Ted Stone looked at Guy incredulously, his voice sharp. "Dwight is your MVP down there! He might be your *only* MVP. Dwight is one of the reasons I bought your company. Why would you want to fire Dwight?"

Here it comes, thought Guy. It was time to see if Argosy really held its values in high esteem.

"Ted, I fired Dwight yesterday."

There was a dangerous look in Ted Stone's eyes that Guy had never seen before, and his voice rose. "You scapegoated him over this!"

"No, that's not true, Ted." Guy held up his hands in what he hoped was a calming manner. "If I was scapegoating Dwight Jones I would be telling this story in a completely different way. Dwight has been a disaster as a supervisor for a long time, and he had no interest in changing. He had little respect for the values we all go by down on Third Street, and he was undermining my authority. This latest incident was part of a pattern that I've ignored for too long."

"I just can't believe you would let such a talent go," Ted responded, his voice hard. "We've got a few insubordinate prima donnas in this place, too, but we figure out ways of handling them." Blame echoed off every syllable.

"Maybe Dwight would fit in here," Guy conceded. "And maybe I should have tried that route first, asked to transfer him here. I could tell you more, about a young woman who called a lawyer after working under Dwight, but this is my responsibility."

Guy sighed, watching rain trace patterns down the window. "Dwight should have been gone long before the merger. I see that now. It's my fault for not seeing it sooner."

"Guy, there might not have been a merger if it weren't for Dwight. Do you understand what I'm saying?"

A faint rumble of thunder punctuated Ted's statement.

Guy was aching inside. He wanted to tell Ted that it was Argosy's values that had helped expose what a destructive force Dwight had been. But now wasn't the right time. Ted would think Guy was using the values as a cover, and he would be right.

Ted continued. "Channeling the talent of an occasional oddball is part of a manager's job, Guy, because there are a lot of talented oddballs in this business, in any business." He looked out the window at a view made hazy by the rain. "If I didn't have the stomach for tolerating the handful of people here whom I strongly suspect have contempt for advertising, contempt for Argosy, heck, contempt for *me*...I wouldn't be here. Argosy wouldn't be here."

Guy held his breath and waited for Ted to finish.

"Okay," Ted said, clearing his throat. He had obviously come to a decision. "What do we do now? Billy Winters over at MegaMart's agency is waiting to hear from us. These should be simple technical matters, but I don't understand them, and I don't know if anyone on Third Street does, either. You've fired the one guy who knows anything at all."

"I will go back and call Billy," Guy said. It was something concrete to do. "I will take down the technical data and consult with Dwight's team. There are at least two specialists we can bring in who have worked with Dwight and understand his designs."

Ted shifted back in his chair. "I'm tempted to ask how everything else is going with the TrekPhone campaign, but that's like, 'So, Mrs. Lincoln, how did you enjoy the play?'" Ted said it in a light falsetto voice, and he smiled for the first time in the conversation. Guy smiled, too, encouraged.

"Don't get me wrong, Guy," Ted said. "I hear what you're saying about Dwight. I even think I hear what you're *not* saying. Maybe it's easier to hide the oddballs in a big place like this one. In your shop it's one floor, one big family—I know it's different."

"Thanks," Guy responded. He didn't know what else to say. For the moment, he was relieved to still have his job.

"No, don't thank me yet," Ted grew stern again. "I'm taking you at your word. This whole debacle is your fault and you've got to pull it out of the fire before it's too late. There are millions of dollars at stake here. So fix it. I don't care how. Just go back, call Billy, and fix it. I'm not going to say whether you made the right move or the wrong move on Dwight, on this, on anything."

Abruptly, he stood and gestured toward the door.

"It's the results, Guy. The results will decide the outcome."

CHAPTER 19

Liberty and Lunch

Guy's ears felt hot during the cab ride back to Third Street. That look on Ted Stone's face, when he'd told Ted that he'd fired Dwight, was seared into Guy's memory. He felt as though a bond had been broken between Ted and himself, and as he watched the rainy cityscape pass, Guy began to choke up. From his first meeting with Ted Stone, the moment he feared the most had arrived.

As he walked through the Third Street office, Guy shot a glance toward Dwight's empty desk. The young programmers and designers in that corner of the office were looking drawn and a little haunted. It was like a death had occurred in the team's family, even if none of them had particularly liked Dwight. Mike, the young man who had mishandled the last call from MegaMart, was looking particularly stricken.

Guy closed his office door and took a moment to think. He asked himself if he had overreacted, if he'd acted precipitously. No. He hadn't. He remembered Stanley's advice: *What harm might Dwight be doing this minute if he was still here?* Stanley was right. The thought helped. But it didn't solve Guy's present difficulties.

Guy put in a call to Billy Winters at MegaMart's agency in Denver. Billy would not be back until 4 p.m., Eastern Time. Guy left a message on his voicemail, promising to call back then.

Lunch was approaching, and Guy decided he needed to do something to shake things up. He suspected that the members of Dwight's team were feeding off of each other's negativity, and he needed to do what he could to halt that progression. For today, anyway, he was still creative director of Eaton/Argosy. Removing Dwight had left his cadre of web developers feeling raw and vulnerable. There wasn't much Guy could do to make things better for them.

But he could feed them. And maybe get to know them a little bit better. That would be a start.

Guy strode over to the web design corner and saw that Mike was missing. "Where's Mike?" he asked the others.

"He ran downstairs to grab a hot dog." There was a street vendor right outside the front door, and it was a popular lunch option among Eaton/Argosy employees.

"Okay," Guy said, bobbing his head and summoning some energy. "Who's up for Morimoto?"

The young designers looked awestruck. "Seriously?" one said. It was a trendy, high-end Japanese restaurant that none of them could afford.

"Yeah, c'mon, let's go," Guy urged them. "And hurry. We need to save Mike from buying that hot dog."

Mike was still in line when they got downstairs, and the morning's rain had started to taper off. "Let's go, Mike!" Guy called. Mike's head jerked around under his umbrella, his eyes darting to see who had called him.

One of the designers was beaming. "Mike. Morimoto!"

The Eaton/Argosy offices in Old City are just blocks away from Independence Hall and the Liberty Bell, which is on public display in a modern glass pavilion. Guy and his crew had to pass by both buildings to get to Morimoto. As they approached the Liberty Bell on the right, they made their way past the long line of tourists snaking its way down Chestnut Street. Guy looked at the bell, and read its inscription for what felt like the thousandth time.

"Proclaim liberty throughout the land."

He read the phrase back to himself. In his vulnerable state this afternoon, he felt like he understood for the first time the profound risk that statement had once represented. Most of the signers of the Declaration of Independence were businesspeople. They ranked among the privileged elite in their corner of the British Empire. They were merchants and landowners who had every excuse for playing it safe and avoiding the Revolutionary cause. And yet they made war on the most powerful empire on earth, even though they could have been hanged for it.

Why had they done it? What moved such sensible men to take such a reckless chance?

It was about values, wasn't it?

The web designers with Guy were trading stories about the nearby nightclubs, and Guy, walking several steps ahead of them, became lost in a brief historic reverie. He considered the Revolution for the first time as a war over how colonial America could live by its own set of core values.

The founding fathers had originally demanded their rights as British subjects, and they wanted the British to live up to the values shared by the English and colonials alike. With the Declaration of Independence, though, the signers laid out a new set of American core values. By putting their names to that document, they committed themselves to either live by those values or die in the effort.

The signers were in the minority. A lot of merchants and landowners either sided with the powerful empire or remained neutral. Some decided it was more noble to remain loyal to the king.

But what honor did that choice win them? None. No one in America trusted the Loyalists once the Revolution was over. Many had to flee to Canada or move back to England after the war.

And is their memory and sacrifice for king and crown honored or revered in Canada or England today? Guy pondered. *No. Because all the things they sought to preserve—their money, their property, their loyalty to the crown—proved to be transient.*

Only values have endured, he thought, with a surge of hope and conviction. *Only values matter.*

Once everyone had settled into the booth at Morimoto, Guy felt that wave of calm certainty come over him, as it had during his tense meeting with Dwight on Values Day. He felt clear now, maybe for the first time in weeks.

"So, who wants to tell me how they're doing today?" he asked the group after they had placed their drink orders. "Dwight's gone, but what I'm really interested in is how everyone is feeling."

"We're okay, I guess," Mike ventured, fiddling with his chopsticks. "I mean, it was kind of a shock. One day Dwight's getting free dinners at Le Bec-Fin, and the next day he's gone."

"I understand," affirmed Guy. "That doesn't seem very consistent, and we all like consistency in the workplace, don't we? Okay. What else?"

"We don't know what's going to happen next, I guess," offered another designer. "And we don't know who our boss is now."

"We're also worried about TrekPhone, about the account," chimed in a third. He didn't sound convincing, but he was at least mindful that the client should still matter in these kinds of discussions.

"Okay," Guy said, sweeping the table with his gaze. "First, I won't tell you why Dwight is gone. It's not fair to him, and it's not the way we do things here. But I will assure you that his leaving has everything to do with supporting the behaviors we identified on Values Day.

"Those behaviors matter," he continued. "They represent a consensus of everyone in our office about how we will live our core values at work. So without saying too much more, I'll assure you that no one who violates these behaviors in our workplace will be comfortable working here for very long."

The faces looking back at Guy around the table were noncommittal. Clearly, no one was convinced.

Guy continued, "No matter how skilled, how talented, or how gifted you are, you won't get a free pass on values as long as I'm the boss. That's my personal promise to you, and to everyone in the office."

Guy explained that he would be counting on their help in the search for a new chief of web design, and that they should consider Linda Hutchinson their supervisor for the time being. They seemed relieved at that news, and it came just as the food arrived.

As far as Guy was concerned, the purpose of the lunch had been accomplished. It was a first step in rebuilding trust among young people who had been treated badly for too long. He would have been happy to sit back, ask them about their lives, and spend the rest of the luncheon getting to know them better.

But all they wanted to talk about was the TrekPhone website. They were all under 30—members of TrekPhone's target demographic. They had some good ideas about what they wanted to see in the site. Dwight had already adopted some of these ideas, but now, for the first time, Guy was hearing about the ones Dwight had rejected.

"You know that feature where you move the cursor over the image of the phone and the features pop out at you?" one of them said. "I kind of suggested that to Dwight, but I wasn't sure how to write the code for it. Dwight was amazing. He did it so fast, and it worked better his way than I thought it would."

"Did he show you how he did it?" Guy asked, curious.

No, he hadn't. No surprise there. He hadn't documented the source files, either, so it would be difficult for anyone else to work on it.

"So if Dwight didn't show you what he was doing, how much trouble are we in with TrekPhone and MegaMart?" Guy asked with trepidation. As Ted had instructed him, he *had* to make this work. "How hard will it be to pick up where Dwight left off?"

"We were talking about that today," Mike responded. He began to explain all the work they had done just that morning. Earlier in the day, Guy had read their faces as withdrawn and worried. He'd been mistaken. They were concentrating.

"It looks like Dwight didn't document any of his source files, so we'll have to run a bunch of tests to figure them out," Mike continued. "Some things we'll just have to throw out and do over. But as long as Linda is there to help us make decisions, we think we can do it."

With that much settled, Guy asked about the retail sign-up feature on the website. This was the feature Ted Stone was so pleased with, the one he wanted Dwight and Guy to show off to the web designers at Argosy headquarters. The code behind it was complicated, but that's all Guy knew about it.

"That page isn't too much of a problem." Mike was in his element now, all traces of uncertainty gone. "Dwight did a lot of custom work there, but we all had a hand in helping him. We might know our way around that page better than most of the other pages Dwight built."

Guy took a bite of chicken teriyaki. "Let's order some desserts to go," he said, to enthusiastic nods of approval.

Maybe, just maybe, this was going to work out after all.

CHAPTER 20

Hire Values. Train Talent.

Guy still had an hour's wait before he could reach Billy Winters in Denver. He looked for something to do while the Mega-Mart deal, and his job, hung in the balance.

Strolling over to Randi's desk, Guy asked if she had a few minutes to talk. Randi, ever enthusiastic, nodded vigorously and hopped out of her chair. When they got to Guy's office, he left the door open as he asked her about the planning for TrekPhone events.

"We've got a bunch of things ready to propose," Randi told him. "We want to do polar bear events with TrekPhones at the zoos in the top dozen media markets. We think we could sponsor recycling promotions and contests in those same markets. And we've got a call into the management for Green Day, the rock group. They might be touring around the time of the launch, and we can do sponsorships and activities to support the tour."

"This all sounds like fun," Guy said, genuinely impressed. The TrekPhone campaign was a completely different ballgame from those of the startups with which Eaton had formerly worked. "It's big league stuff, isn't it?"

"The possibilities are endless, and I've never had a budget like this before." Randi seemed genuinely happy.

"How are you doing with what we talked about a few weeks back, your professional development?"

"Oh, it's good," she said crossing her legs and leaning forward. "I've signed up for a project management course, and I've asked Linda to go over the materials with me. And your suggestion that I start going to the luncheons at the events planning association was a really good one. The first one was fun, and I made some really great contacts."

"Just don't run off and get hired by any of them," Guy kidded her. "Not now anyway." Then Guy asked about her Personal Leadership Philosophy. She still hadn't finished it.

"I don't know," she said, her eyebrows drawing together. "I'm still kind of blocked on that. When I try to write it, I feel silly. Not that it's a silly thing to do. It's me. I guess I don't feel like a leader."

"You have my PLP, right?" Guy asked her. "What I want you to do is ask Linda and Andy to give you theirs. Then here's what you do. Make it a cut and paste job, plain and simple. Just copy from us every promise you think your team needs to get from you. Copy every expectation you have that they should know about. Copy every hot button...."

"I don't think I have any hot buttons."

Although Randi was understanding and helpful almost to a fault, Guy doubted that was true.

"You don't like being lied to or having things kept from you, do you? So put it in there. There are no points for originality in this. The key thing is...."

She interrupted him, "That I'm living the values. I know. My team should know what to expect and what's expected from them. Okay. I'll get it done." Guy thanked her and she went back to her desk.

Guy looked at the clock. Fifteen minutes until Billy Winters would be back from lunch. He thought about Randi for a moment, and he remembered something Stanley Sabato had told him. If your people accept the values, you can help them develop their skills. But for those who reject the values, there's no help for them, no matter how many technical skills they bring to their jobs. Their behavior will always undermine their effectiveness.

For all of Dwight's natural talent, it was impossible to bring him around on his behavior. His talent—and everything it produced—suffered as a result. Randi, by contrast, was eager to develop her skills. Why? Because of her attitude. She was ready to live the values.

With that in mind, Guy grabbed a sticky note and rushed to scribble something down before the thought had a chance to pass:

"Hire values. Train talent."

He opened his file drawer and took out the folder marked "Director of Web Design." He placed the sticky note on the page with the heading "job description." Those words would guide him as he looked for someone who would be a true asset to the Eaton/Argosy team.

CHAPTER 21

Problem Children

When Billy Winters finally returned Guy's call at 4:18 p.m., he proved to be of no help.

"I don't know who your web people were dealing with at MegaMart," he said with a hint of impatience in his voice. "I can give you my contact there. That's probably the best I can do for you."

Guy took the name and number Billy gave him. Then he called Arnie Mann for advice. He felt that he had to handle MegaMart with kid gloves at this point. Calling someone new and dragging him into it didn't seem like such a good idea.

"You should go ahead and call the web designer that Mike and Dwight were fighting with," Arnie said without hesitation after Guy filled him in. "I'll call him, if you want."

"No, I'll call," Guy replied. "We need to deal with these technical problems from this office, so I'll just call him and ask for another chance."

"That's very humble, Guy," Arnie said, pausing for a second before "humble."

Guy couldn't tell if Arnie was mocking him or not.

"Just remember that this is a multi-million-dollar deal and he's just a techie. He can't kill a deal like this just because he's got a grudge." Arnie seemed more certain of that fact than Guy himself was.

"I know, but if he's mad enough he can try," said Guy, imagining a worst-case scenario. "If he's really fed up with us, he can put a scare into his managers. He'll say, 'Oh, if we link to this TrekPhone page the way they want us to, the whole Mega-Mart site could crash.' His bosses would probably say, 'Let's just pass.'"

Arnie lowered his voice, ignoring Guy's doomsday scenario. "Hey, Guy, I cannot *believe* you fired Dwight Jones after Ted sent him a dinner from Le Bec-Fin. Everyone's talking about it."

"They are?" Guy chewed the inside of his lip. After that morning's meeting with Ted, mention of Dwight made him nervous.

"You'll probably get away with it because you're new," Arnie told him. "But no one fires the star performers around here. You need to know that."

"Ted told me he's got a few prima donnas there, but he didn't say they were fireproof." This was not encouraging news. Guy began to swivel back and forth in his chair as he listened to Arnie talk.

"They're treated like milk-fed veal," Arnie's voice lowered yet again. "Some of us call them the Problem Children. It might as well be a job category here, like manager or secretary."

"Ted said everyone learns how to handle them."

Arnie was silent for a long moment. "Ted has no idea." The scandalized exuberance was no longer present in his voice.

"He doesn't?" This was the first time Guy had heard Ted criticized so bluntly.

"It's unbelievable, some of the behavior we tolerate. And some of it comes from people who haven't done anything worthwhile in years. They spend their time cultivating their images as creative geniuses, and avoid doing any serious work. It can get pretty demoralizing." Arnie finished with a sigh.

Guy stopped swiveling, digesting this new piece of information. "Ted doesn't know this?"

"You've seen the size of this place," Arnie replied. "Every project manager is under pressure to produce results. The less Ted knows about how things actually get done, the happier he is. Ted wants steak. Don't bore him with details about how the cow got slaughtered."

"But he's been right on top of me ever since he bought us," Guy said, confused. He felt as though his every move had been weighed and measured since the merger.

"It's different for you right now, because you're a recent acquisition. Eaton is a new toy, and Ted wants to wind it up and see how it works. You're under the microscope for now. That's why this thing with Dwight was such bad timing."

"He had to go, Arnie," Guy said, lacking the energy to defend himself any further. "Can you believe me on that?"

"More power to you," Arnie replied. "I'm waiting to see how it works out. If you get away with it, maybe I'll try to put one of my own Problem Children out the door."

Guy thanked Arnie for his advice on the MegaMart call. "If you don't mind, I'm going to drop you an email about it, you know, that you said I should just call Dwight and Mike's contact at MegaMart."

"An email?" Arnie sounded wary.

"Helps me remember things," Guy said, shrugging.

What Guy remembered was how Arnie and his people had shifted the blame to Eaton/Argosy for the delay in the Trek-Phone campaign makeover. Arnie had sandbagged him once. Guy wasn't going to let him do it again.

CHAPTER 22

Communication Restored

MegaMart Online was based on the West Coast, so Guy stayed late and waited for the Eaton/Argosy office to quiet down before he dialed the number of Nelson Winsick, the MegaMart web designer with whom Dwight and Mike had quarreled. Late afternoon sunlight slanted into Guy's office as he waited for Nelson to pick up.

The phone rang six times before Guy heard a gravelly voice on the other end of the line.

"Winsick."

"Nelson, this is Guy Cedrick at Eaton/Argosy. I work on the TrekPhone website with Dwight and Mike."

"Yes." Nelson's voice was distant and robotic. He was not going to make this easy, and Guy supposed he had a good reason for being taciturn.

"I'm calling for two reasons," Guy said. "First, I want to apologize. I'm Dwight and Mike's boss, and I hear you haven't been treated well. I want to assure you that it won't happen again."

"Okay. Thank you." Then more silence.

"The second reason I'm calling is to tell you that Dwight Jones is no longer with Eaton/Argosy...." Guy's voice trailed off. He didn't want to get into the details of Dwight's departure.

"He what?" Nelson's voice was beginning to sound a little less forced.

"He's no longer here," Guy repeated. "And I know that might pose additional problems for our work together. So I want to assure you that this is getting my full, personal attention."

"Did Dwight get fired?" Nelson sounded incredulous.

"That's...an internal matter," Guy said, choosing his words carefully. "But you should know this. We have some core values around here, like respect, integrity, and communication. It's safe to say that everyone you contact from this office now fully grasps the importance of those values."

"You know, the problems we're having aren't all that complicated," Nelson said. Now he was the one who sounded apologetic. "But I felt like I was going in circles with Mike and Dwight, and I've got a lot on my plate here." He drew a long breath. "I hung up on Mike. That wasn't very respectful or professional, either."

"Thanks for saying that," Guy said, truly appreciative of Nelson's honesty. "But Mike was probably being uncooperative because he was under Dwight's direction. I need to ask you a favor, Nelson. I need you to pick up where you left off with Mike, if that's okay with you."

"Sure. Absolutely. I was just waiting for you guys to get back in touch."

"Mike gave me your email," Guy told him. "I'm going to send you my cell phone number, and because you're on the West Coast, I'll give you my home number, too. If anything comes up that you think is more than Mike can handle, I want you to call me. And again, my apologies for what happened before."

"That's okay, Guy. I'll talk to Mike in the morning. Thanks."

Guy put down the receiver and reflected back on the conversation. Nelson had been guarded and defensive at the start of the call. His tone had become agreeable only after Guy had offered an apology and learned that Guy had taken decisive action.

Guy realized that this call was one of the tests Stanley had told him about. With a billion dollars on the line, Guy felt he'd passed. He closed his blinds, grabbed his briefcase, flicked his lights off, and headed home.

Overall, the day hadn't been as bad as he'd feared. In fact, he was starting to feel pretty good about this putting-it-all-on-the-line-for-values thing.

CHAPTER 23

The Truth About Values

For the next ten days, Guy heard almost nothing from Ted Stone. Mike was still working around Nelson's busy schedule at MegaMart Online to resolve the web glitches between the TrekPhone webpage and the MegaMart site. Then one day Mike sprang into Guy's office.

"We've got it working! It's on a password-protected beta-site. Here are the codes." He placed a piece of paper on Guy's desk with a flourish.

"Should I pass these codes on to Ted and Arnie?" Guy asked. He suppressed a grin at Mike's transformation from subdued flunky to eager team player.

Mike suggested that Guy take a few minutes to inspect the beta-site himself, and Guy followed his advice.

The TrekPhone page looked different. Some of Dwight's technical flourishes were gone, and Guy assumed that they had been the root cause of the compatibility problems all along. MegaMart's website had a simple design to accommodate moderate-income shoppers with slower Internet access and older computers. Guy could now see that Dwight had been trying to park a Ferrari in a lot filled with Chevys.

Feeling good about what his team had accomplished against the odds, Guy wrote Arnie and Ted an email: *The TrekPhone page on MegaMart Online is testing well. Codes for access to the beta-test site are attached.*

An hour later, Guy's BlackBerry buzzed.

G-

Looks good. Let's catch up this afternoon. 4 p.m.

Ted

The MegaMart Online page was open on Ted Stone's computer when Guy entered his office.

"This looks very good," Ted said after Guy had taken a seat.

Guy could hear genuine admiration in the older man's voice.

"Do you realize what a big step this is?" Ted asked. "Our client will be the first company ever with its own guest page on the MegaMart site! It's going to get written up in the business magazines. They're going to study the results in business schools." His voice took on a dreamy tone.

"That's what Arnie tells me." Guy tried to tamp down the pride in his voice, but it was a difficult task. As he'd been reminded time and time again, Ted Stone didn't hand out praise willy-nilly.

"And what I can't get out of my head is that Dwight Jones' design inspired it. Got the whole thing rolling. And now he's lost to us." Clearly, Ted had come back down to earth.

Guy's heart sank. The ghost of Dwight was still in the room.

"Did you know that he won't return Arnie's calls?" Ted asked. "I suggested we try to work with him as a freelancer, but he won't call Arnie back. He hasn't been to Le Bec-Fin, either. I checked."

"He may need some time," Guy said, trying to be diplomatic. Ted's news didn't surprise him in the least, though, and he doubted that Dwight would even redeem his gift certificate. Dwight was definitely the type to cut off his nose to spite his face.

"Maybe," Ted said. He didn't sound convinced, either. Ted pushed a fat file folder across his desk toward Guy. "I asked our human relations department to run off copies of all the resumes that might fit Dwight's job description. We did some hiring recently and we turned down some strong candidates we didn't have room for."

"Thanks." Guy recognized the resumes as the veiled peace offering they were.

"Yeah, well, once you get someone new in there, we can finally see whether you made the right move when you fired Dwight," Ted said, looking sideways at Guy.

"Ted, I'd like to say something about that," Guy began. He held Stanley's advice in mind. Now it was time for Ted Stone to walk the plank.

"This was the right move for Eaton/Argosy," Guy stated. "Down on Third Street, we have Argosy and its core values to thank for it."

"What are you talking about?" Ted frowned at Guy, resting his temple on the first two fingers of his right hand.

"If you remember the first time I came to see you here, you asked me if the Eaton Group was ready to play at Argosy's level. You wanted to know how the people on Third Street would take to the Argosy company purpose and core values," Guy explained.

Ted gave a single nod. "I remember."

"And I remember telling you that some would be turned off right away, but that others might want to wait and see if the leadership was living up to those values before they were ready to take them seriously." Guy didn't name names, but he hoped he'd made his meaning apparent.

"What's this got to do with firing Dwight?"

Apparently Guy would have to make his point a bit more clearly. He took a deep breath, and started speaking again. "Everything, Ted. Dwight had a cynical attitude about Argosy's core values right from the start. When the TrekPhone project came to us the way it did, he was the first to denigrate Argosy for the way it was handled."

Ted got defensive. "What was wrong with the way things were handled?"

Guy measured his words carefully. "I saw TrekPhone immediately as a huge opportunity. But for the rest of the staff, it came as a shock to have the directions handed to them, without being able to talk to anyone at TrekPhone. They're used to working with clients and developing the strategy, from the bottom up. This was a top-down approach, with no apology or explanation. And while Linda and I tried to be positive about it, Dwight was the ringleader for negativity."

"That account is a privilege to work on," Ted said, his voice a bit heated. "Do you have any idea how disappointed some of my marketing people were when I decided to gave TrekPhone to your shop?"

Guy paused. He had to make his point without offending Ted. "I understand that, Ted," he began. "But if you asked me how I would have handled it, if the shoe were on the other foot, I would have brought Third Street in on the conversations sooner. I would have involved them in the process. At the very least, I would have explained more fully why involving them earlier hadn't been an option."

"It wasn't an option!" Ted's jaw was clenched.

"You're asking me, Ted, so I'm telling you." Guy hoped he could placate his boss. "With the TrekPhone assignment, I don't feel like Third Street was treated with Argosy's core values in mind. Respect, integrity, and communication were all lacking, and excellence suffered as a result. I had a demoralized staff.

They were doing very professional work on TrekPhone, but they were growing cynical about the values and about me and my leadership. That's when I decided we needed to hold a Values Day, which was the beginning of the end for Dwight."

Guy explained his history with Stanley and how he had adopted the Navy practice of Values Days by holding one on Third Street. After that day, he said, tolerating Dwight was no longer possible. If Guy wanted to maintain any credibility with the rest of the staff, Dwight had to go.

"This whole experience has changed my ideas about talent," Guy admitted. "We have a number of people at Third Street whom I always thought were very good. But because they didn't have Dwight's obvious brilliance, I've underestimated what many of our people are capable of. I'm looking at them now with an eye toward stretching them, getting them outside training, giving them new experiences. You know why? Because I see them living our core values and responding to that list of behaviors they all helped develop.

"Dwight's gone, and we'll miss his talent, no doubt. But our overall capability is much greater without him," Guy finished, clasping his hands tightly in his lap.

While Guy was talking, he saw Ted's eyes get a brief faraway look, as though he'd just been reminded of something. Now an uncomfortable pause settled between the two men.

"Let me ask your advice on something," Ted finally said, catching Guy's gaze. "Let's say I catch someone shading the truth here and there, keeping things from me. Someone close to me, someone on whom I rely. What should I do, fire him for not living the values? Even though this is someone who always comes through for me?"

Guy got the distinct impression Ted was talking about Arnie Mann, and he felt honored that Ted was asking for his advice, even if it was in a roundabout way. "You're asking me what I'd do about someone like that?"

"Yes. I'm very curious."

"I'd start by looking at myself," Guy said after thinking for a few seconds. "I'd wonder if I were somehow inviting this person to manipulate me because he hasn't felt safe being truthful. I told you about my Personal Leadership Philosophy. I put it right in there. Bring me bad news when it's fresh, when we can still act on it. Everyone who works with me is on notice that there's no excuse for going behind my back. But that's because I've assured them in writing that I won't kill the messenger."

"Do you think I'm one of those guys who kills the messenger?" One corner of Ted's mouth quirked up in a half-smile.

"No," Guy responded, smiling back. "But for all I know, that might be part of the culture here. As Stanley explained to me...."

"Stanley, the submarine captain," Ted interrupted.

"Yes, that's right. Stanley said that the purpose of Values Day in the Navy was to get the crew to associate the department's core values with the behaviors they would all like to see every day—like communicating clearly and feeling free to deliver bad news. Values Day can bring shipmates—and officemates—a sense of a shared culture, defined by values that are backed up with specific behaviors. Unless everyone knows those behaviors, the values can seem like hollow words, and the workplace can get cynical about them."

Ted looked skeptical. "I don't know, Guy. Is my behavior so out of whack with the values here?" His face softened a bit. "What bad news are you afraid to tell me?"

Guy smiled again. "There is one small thing that I have never found the right time to tell you about," he said. "Do you want to hear it?"

"Yes! What is it?"

"Your biography on the company website has a quote from you that erroneously defines the word 'argosy.'"

"It what?" Ted's eyebrows rose.

"You say in the biography that an argosy is a journey. But it's not. It's a fleet of ships."

"How do you know that?" Now Ted looked incredulous.

"It's easy enough to find," Guy replied. "It turns up in any web search."

Ted spun to his computer and looked up "argosy." With his back to Guy, he waited a moment and then he muttered, "This is so embarrassing."

"It's an easy mistake to make," Guy offered. After all, he hadn't realized the error until Stanley had pointed it out to him.

"Yeah, but I didn't even make it," Ted said. He got up and walked to a side table with glasses and a pitcher of water. "One of the copywriters here put this together."

A copywriter who obviously didn't bother doing a quick online dictionary check, thought Guy. "So that's not really how you came up with the name Argosy?" he asked.

Ted looked over his shoulder at Guy, then turned back around and poured two glasses of water. "Very few people know this, but 'Argosy' is an inside joke," Ted replied, walking back over to his desk and handing Guy one of the glasses. "Nick Argos is one of the silent partners here. He put up most of the money for our big merger ten years ago. I promised to name the new company after him. Hardly anyone here even knows who he is."

Ted looked back at the Argosy definition on his computer screen. "How many people here knew about this and didn't tell me?" Ted asked. Guy assumed it was a rhetorical question and said nothing.

Ted finished reading the whole entry and then was silent for a moment.

"Okay," he said, opening the fat file folder in front of him. "Before you go, Stella in human relations flagged some of the better candidates for you. I'm going to take a second here to check off the ones I think can do Dwight's job. You can ask me about them later if any make your first cut." He checked off a few of the resumes, then handed the folder to Guy.

"Do you need anything else from me?" Ted asked.

"No," said Guy with a smile. "Thanks for hearing me out."

"Sure, sure," Ted said. He stood up to escort Guy out the door. "I'm still thinking about this, and I'm not sure how much I can go along with. But do me a favor. Before you leave today, send me a copy of your Personal Leadership Plan...." His voice trailed off.

"The PLP."

"Yeah, get me a copy of that right away. And have someone fax or email that list of behaviors you all came up with on your Values Day." Ted shook Guy's hand.

"I paid for that consulting group to give us those four values," he continued. "Now I hear you say that maybe there's more there than we thought. So I'm curious to see what Third Street managed to do with the core values. Maybe we still haven't gotten our money's worth from the exercise."

As Guy rode the elevator back down to the lobby, he allowed himself a private grin. Argosy hadn't walked off the edge of the plank after all.

CHAPTER 24

A Lesson Learned

The following Sunday afternoon, Guy and Melanie were barbequing in the backyard while the girls played in the sandbox by the swing set. On the other side of the privacy hedge, they could hear Stanley Sabato using power tools on his summer-long boat-building project. All in all, Guy felt more relaxed than he had in a long while.

Melanie had brought Molly's high chair out into the yard and Guy left his keys and his BlackBerry on the plastic high chair tray. Suddenly the BlackBerry sprang to life. It did a vibrating dance across the tray, rattling Guy's keys.

There was a text message from Ted Stone.

"R U and your sub captain free for lunch this week? RE: Argosy Values Day."

Ted Stone didn't know it, but he had passed Guy Cedrick's last test.

"Hey, Stanley," Guy called over the hedge, "are you up for having a big steak with Ted Stone and me this week?"

"Steak?" Stanley called back over the sound of his drill. "Always."

Guy puzzled for a moment how to phrase the text reply. He started with, "We're happy to do it," and then stopped and deleted the sentence.

"Looking forward to it," he began again, then frowned and cleared his screen again.

Then he thought: *the less said, the better.* Ted Stone had signaled that he was willing to learn from Guy. Guy should show Ted that he was learning, too.

Guy hit three buttons and sent the message:

"Yes."

The Focus and Alignment Workshop: Helping Real-Life Organizations Set Their Own Core Values Compass

The day-long values exercise through which Guy Cedrick leads his team in Chapters 8-11 is based on one portion of a real-life two-day seminar developed by Academy Leadership. It's called the "Focus and Alignment Workshop" and it's designed to guide companies into the future and provide common threads for developing leaders.

As with Guy Cedrick's employer, organizations with purpose statements and a set of core values rarely take the time to determine how their policies, procedures, and behaviors could be better aligned with these espoused ideals. We see in Argosy a typical company that operates far below its potential due to executive-level dysfunction. Immediate short-term performance is the only value that truly matters to the company. The lip-service paid by Argosy's leaders to their corporate purpose and values merely contributes to a cynical workplace culture.

The Focus and Alignment Workshop is designed to help executive teams avoid Argosy's problems by taking a longer view and creating a healthier, more effective organization. Workshop participants develop a plan that enables nearer-term goals to be expressed in ways consistent with the company's mission, vision, values, and overarching purpose. By setting a course for the future in this way, executive teams can also build up their own internal strength and cohesion. The ultimate outcome? Enhanced organizational performance.

In their bestselling book *Built to Last: Successful Habits of Visionary Companies*, Jim Collins and Jerry I. Porras show how companies with exceptional long-term performance in a wide variety of industries all share the "focus and alignment" practice. Companies that regularly out-perform their peers each have a core ideology that consists of an organizational purpose statement and a set of core values. Everyone in these companies knows and understands these concepts, because time and resources are devoted toward ensuring that day-to-day activities and immediate business objectives are all in alignment with them.

If getting people to this point sounds like an arduous and time-consuming task, consider for a moment the difficulties that arise when everyone on a team nurtures his or her own concept of how to interpret the organization's purpose and values statements. Throw in the few cases of employees who ignore or openly violate that core ideology, and you might easily conclude that having no core ideology at all would be preferable to having one that is disrespected and not enforced.

In the Focus and Alignment Workshop, we divide executive team members into small groups and ask them to define their fundamental expectations for workplace behavior. This is how they begin to identify the core values of the organization. The values should describe how members of the organization should operate on a daily basis as they pursue the organization's purpose.

We bring the groups back together, and in a plenary session they hash out which of all the proposed values truly reside at the organization's ideological core. The list needs to be short to be effective. The best companies have at least three but no more than five core values.

Once each value has been defined in general terms, it needs to be described more fully in terms of outward behavior: i.e., *If I act in line with our values, what would an observer see me doing?* We send everyone back to their small groups with an assignment to generate three to five normative behavioral statements for one or more of the proposed core values.

As we saw with Guy Cedrick and his team at Argosy, even after "communication" was accepted by the larger group as a core value, at least one individual disputed its inclusion on the list. But once a set of specific, reasonable behaviors was attached to that value, there was no question that a new, higher standard for normative behavior in that office had been set.

The final step is probably the most uncomfortable one, which often makes it the most worthwhile. Members of the small groups are asked to consider which of their company's existing policies or common practices are inconsistent with these newly identified core values. Then the group needs to determine what should be done about the inconsistency. What corrective action needs to be taken to align behavior with the organization's values?

It's hard to overstate the importance of such an exercise. By the end of the second day, workshop participants have come to a common agreement on where they want their company to go for the next ten years or more. They know the major action steps necessary to achieve this common vision, and they know who within the senior executive management team is accountable for each one. Without this shared understanding of values, aligned with purpose, policies, and practices, an organization is destined for mediocrity at best.

The Focus and Alignment Workshop operates from a strict hierarchy of guideposts in which only the very purpose of the organization itself ranks more highly than values. We find that vision statements, mission statements, goals, and objectives are all dependent on the organization's values—how its members are expected to treat customers, the community, and each other. When it comes time for planning and goal-setting, focus is derived from the alignment of core values with behavior. In the absence of alignment, focus always remains elusive.

To learn more about Academy Leadership programs, please call us at 866-783-0630 or visit our website: www.academyleadership. com.

The Core Values Compass
Self-Evaluation Questionnaire

How well have you and your work unit established focus and alignment with your company's purpose, values, vision, mission, and goals? Respond to the following statements by marking the options closest to your current situation. Be as honest as you can.

Options			
1. Strongly Disagree	2. Disagree	3. Agree	4. Strongly Agree

1. I know what my company's Purpose Statement says.
   ☐1 ☐2 ☐3 ☐4

2. I understand my company's Purpose Statement.
   ☐1 ☐2 ☐3 ☐4

3. My organization's Purpose Statement means something to me and inspires me.
   ☐1 ☐2 ☐3 ☐4

4. I have discussed the company's Purpose Statement with people who report to me.
   ☐1 ☐2 ☐3 ☐4

5. The people who report to me understand our company's Purpose Statement.
   ☐1 ☐2 ☐3 ☐4

6. I know our company's Core Values.

   1   2   3   4

7. I understand the definitions of our Core Values.

   1   2   3   4

8. I have discussed the company's Core Values statement with people who report to me.

   1   2   3   4

9. The people who report to me understand the company's Core Values.

   1   2   3   4

10. The people who report to me have suggested additional normative behavioral statements for value consistency.

    1   2   3   4

11. I know our company's Ten-Year Vision.

    1   2   3   4

12. I understand our company's Ten-Year Vision.

    1   2   3   4

13. I have discussed our Ten-Year Vision statement with people who report to me.

    1   2   3   4

14. The people who report to me understand our Ten-Year Vision statement.

    1   2   3   4

15. Our company's Ten-Year Vision statement serves as a clear guide to where our company should be in the future.

    ☐ 1   ☐ 2   ☐ 3   ☐ 4

16. I know the long-term goals (Key Performance Indicators) that must be achieved in order for our company to reach its Ten-Year Vision.

    ☐ 1   ☐ 2   ☐ 3   ☐ 4

17. I know the goals that our company plans to achieve this year.

    ☐ 1   ☐ 2   ☐ 3   ☐ 4

18. I understand the goals that we plan to achieve this year.

    ☐ 1   ☐ 2   ☐ 3   ☐ 4

19. I have discussed our company goals for this year with people who report to me.

    ☐ 1   ☐ 2   ☐ 3   ☐ 4

20. The people who report to me and I have identified the company goals that we can contribute to.

    ☐ 1   ☐ 2   ☐ 3   ☐ 4

Analysis

Add your total score and check your performance by reading the corresponding evaluation. Look at your areas of strength and think of ways to sustain them, or even improve. Identify your areas needing improvement, and set some specific personal goals for achieving it.

20 – 39:	You probably have not spent sufficient time trying to understand the company's purpose, values, vision, mission, and goals. It will be very difficult for you to provide purpose, direction, and motivation for your work unit. Begin now to gain clarity. Consult with the person you report to in order to gain greater clarity.
40 – 59:	You are basically aware of the company's ideology and plans for the future. However, there appears to be significant room for greater clarity on your part. Clear these ambiguities with the person to whom you report.
60 – 80:	You are fully aware of what the company stands for, considers important, where it wants to go, and how it plans to proceed. Share this with your work unit to ensure that they are as aware as you are. This is important leader business.

What I Will Do Differently

For every item you wish to change, list the actions that you will take to improve.

ITEM	ACTIONS TO IMPROVE

Creating Your Personal Leadership Philosophy

If you've read the previous title in this series, *The Leader's Compass*, you're quite familiar with the Personal Leadership Philosophy (PLP). The book depicted Guy Cedrick in an earlier phase in his career, when he first came to understand that he needed lessons in leadership, not management. Central to his success as a front-line leader was his decision to write a Personal Leadership Philosophy (PLP) and distribute it to his team members.

The Core Values Compass makes reference several times to Guy's PLP as a personal compass to help him navigate the new terrain at Argosy, but it doesn't go into details. For those who haven't read *The Leader's Compass*, here's a brief recap.

The U.S. Army and U.S. Navy both require new commanders to write and distribute a PLP. This document is the leader's explicit statement of standards and expectations. It provides subordinates with general guidance on what to do and how to do it. It also tells them: This is where I stand; this is what I want.

Most important of all, the PLP puts the leader on the spot. It challenges the leader to live by the standards he or she sets out in the document. Thanks to the PLP, every military commander learns very soon that if his or her actions are consistent with the PLP, subordinates will come to trust their commander. This trust is like a deep well of goodwill that the best commanders draw upon when things get tough.

On the other hand, inconsistent behavior by a leader frustrates and confuses subordinates. It sows distrust and even fear. Mixed signals create muddied goals. Workers hesitate to take the initiative if they cannot predict with some reliability how a leader will act or react. Time, money, and effort are wasted by false starts and miscommunications in the absence of clear guidance.

The best way to start writing your own PLP is to think of the best and worst leaders for whom you've ever worked and try to write down the defining qualities that distinguish them from each other. Then look at yourself. Pick the three or four qualities from this list that most closely describe your own leadership style and personality. What underlying values do those qualities embody? What ethical *rules* might you draw from them?

Using these rules, write down the leadership principles you admire in others and wish to model yourself. Write them in the form of "I am" or "I will" statements, since they describe what you aspire to be. As a final step, write down your personal likes and dislikes, the "hot button" issues that are your prerogative as a leader, but *only* if you are consistent in abiding by them yourself. Hot button examples from Guy Cedrick's PLP include, "Don't gossip," "Don't whine," "Don't just point out problems; propose solutions."

You should distribute your PLP to your subordinates only after you have taken some time with it, and perhaps let it sit for a week before making final revisions. Just like a compass, a PLP can keep you on course and provide direction during those inevitable times when you will feel lost, confused, tired, or afraid.

To more fully appreciate the potential of having your own PLP, and for more explicit guidance on how to write one, we recommend that you read *The Leader's Compass* and the materials in the back of that book. For readers of this book, we reprint in full the PLP distributed by Bob McDonald, the truly visionary CEO of Procter & Gamble Company. His is a pretty good example to follow.

What I Believe In

By Robert A. McDonald
CEO, Procter & Gamble Co.

Throughout my education, military, and business careers, there are a few principles in which I believe deeply that drive my behavior every day.

1. Living a life driven by purpose is more meaningful and rewarding than meandering through life without direction. My life's purpose is to improve lives. This operates on many levels. I work to improve the lives of the 6.5 billion people in the world with P&G brands, and I work every day to have a positive impact in the life of just one person. This life goal led me to be a Boy Scout when I was young, to attend West Point and become an officer in the U.S. Army, and to join The Procter & Gamble Company. People like to work for leaders who operate with a clear and consistent purpose. The leader's job is to understand and enable the purpose and dreams of their employees. In this sense the task of the leader becomes a calling, a profession—not a job.

2. Everyone wants to succeed, and success is contagious. I have never in all my life, in any career, in any country, at any time, met a person who tries to fail. Everyone I have met wants to succeed. So the job of the leader is to help people succeed. A leader's job is to catch people succeeding, even if the success is a small one, and to use that small success to build a virtuous cycle of ever larger successes. Since success is contagious, one success will always lead to another, and one successful person will always influence another to be successful. Our job as leaders is to start the fire that fuels the virtuous cycle of success.

3. Putting people in the right jobs is one of the most important jobs of the leader. People like to do work that they are good at. Think about your education. What was your favorite class? What was your grade in that class? Chances are that the class you liked the most was also the one in which you received the best grade. That is not an accident. Human beings always gravitate to things they do well. So our job as leaders is to identify what our people do well, and then to put them into jobs that take advantage of that strength. I personally do not believe in the concept of putting someone in a job to build an "opportunity for improvement." That hurts the individual as they will be unhappy, and hurts the organization as we underutilize the person's talent.

4. Character is the most important trait of a leader. At West Point I learned that the character of a leader is their most important attribute. Character is defined as always putting the needs of the organization above your own. As a captain in the Army, I always ate after the soldiers in my command. At P&G the leader should always take personal responsibility for the results of their organization. As a West Point plebe (freshman)

I learned that I was permitted only four answers: yes, no, no excuse, and I do not understand. These four answers are about character; there is no opportunity for equivocation or excuse; there is no "but."

At West Point I also learned to "choose the harder right instead of the easier wrong." This powerful line comes from the West Point Cadet Prayer. Have you ever noticed how it is easier to do wrong things than right things? A leader who lives by his or her word can be counted on to do the unpopular thing when it is right. To always follow "the harder right," a leader must truly believe that a life directed by moral guidelines promises deeper and richer satisfaction than a self-serving, self-absorbed life. Living up to this ideal of character requires courage, determination, integrity, and self-discipline. You must live by your word and actions, and know that is the most powerful demonstration of leadership.

5. Diverse groups of people are more innovative than homogenous groups. Diversity is a necessity at P&G to reflect the consumers we serve and to drive innovation, one of our five core strengths. Innovation is the result of connections and collaboration. James Burke, science historian and author/producer of *Connections*, documented that innovation often comes from connecting two seemingly disconnected ideas. A diverse group is better able to make these connections since they have a greater diversity of nodes to connect. The role of the leader is to create the environment for connections and collaboration to occur.

Leaders of the most effective diverse teams follow the "Platinum Rule": Treat others as they want to be treated. The leader should know the people he or she works with well enough to know how they want to be treated.

6. Ineffective systems and cultures are bigger barriers to achievement than the talents of people. In Total Quality training we all learned how difficult it was to pick up the right proportion of red and blue beads if the device we were using to pick them up was rigged to get a bad result. Similarly, Peter Senge teaches in his best-selling book *The Fifth Discipline* "structure influences behavior," and systems often result in unintended consequences—like rent controls in New York to help the poor who lived in sub-standard housing actually further reduced investment to upgrade the housing, hurting the people the rent controls were designed to help. The role of the leader is to improve the systems and the culture in which their organization operates to improve the consistency and level of success of the results. Any High Performance Organization must have four components: passionate leadership, sound strategies, robust systems, and a high performance culture. A leader needs to work on all four pillars.

7. There will be some people in the organization who will not make it on the journey. Even after taking all of the steps above, there still will be some people in the leader's organization who will be either unwilling or unable to go on the journey of growth with the leader and the organization. It could be the sales manager who thinks you took away his job by eliminating price/volume negotiation by getting rid of temporary price reduction. Or it could be the individual who it is impossible to find the right job for. A clue to finding these individuals is to find who is not happy day-to-day. It is the leader's job to identify those who cannot go on the journey, help them recognize the tension, and help them identify other careers which offer greater promise.

8. Organizations must renew themselves. Any organization, as with any organism, which is growing must renew itself. Growth by definition requires change. Change requires renewal. The standards of performance which are acceptable today will be unacceptable tomorrow if the organization is growing and improving. As such, the leader must provide training and development opportunities for the individuals in the organization to grow. Renewal is particularly important in a "promote from within" company like P&G. We need a healthy level of attrition within P&G to provide future opportunities for growth for our more junior employees.

9. Recruiting is a top priority. There is nothing more important than recruiting. When we recruit we are hiring the future leaders of the company and also our future friends. It is the source of growth of the company as we continually hire more talented people over time. The leader needs to be active in recruiting to ensure we are constantly raising standards and to gauge the level of renewal of the organization.

10. The true test of the leader is the performance of the organization when they are absent or after they depart. The leader's job is to build sufficient organization capability, including the leadership and individual initiative of the members of the organization as well as the strategies/systems/culture of the organization, so that the leader's presence or absence would not significantly affect the business results. This means that the organization will be able to sustain itself successfully over time regardless of the quality of the leader.

ACADEMY LEADERSHIP SERVICES: DEVELOPING LEADERS YOUR PEOPLE WANT TO FOLLOW

In business, good management is about more than technical competency. To be truly successful, managers must also be leaders. That means having the ability to motivate and direct others toward achieving organizational goals. An effective leadership development program not only conveys those important lessons to participants but also shows them how to train their team members to do the same.

At Academy Leadership, we work with your organization to transform managers at all levels into effective leaders who can energize others to accomplish corporate objectives and create tangible business results.

Based on the leadership principles its founders learned at the Naval Academy and West Point—a passion to lead others, a persistence and drive to win, a focus on integrity, and the importance of clarifying each individual's contribution to the overall mission—Academy Leadership training, seminar, and keynote opportunities provide you and your staff with the essential skills you need to achieve business success.

Great leadership skills are at the pinnacle of what drives corporations to succeed. The best way to hardwire these leadership practices at your organization is through extensive and consistent training and leadership development. Read on to learn more about what Academy Leadership has to offer!

The Leadership Boot Camp Experience

An intensive three-day leadership skills training program led by former corporate executives and service academy graduates, the Leadership Boot Camp Experience is designed to transform your managers into leaders. This small-group seminar (limited to 15 people per session) shows your team how to improve business results by becoming better leaders. All who participate will come away more confident, more productive, more in-command, and better able to get things done through other people.

This is your team's chance to learn leadership *as it is taught at West Point and the Naval Academy* to the world's most successful military officers and future business leaders! The management and leadership skills taught at Leadership Boot Camp are based on military academy leadership principles and were developed and tested by an elite group of ex-military-officers-turned-entrepreneurs-and-CEOs. They have been battle-tested in the real world and are sure to generate real results for participants.

Send your organization's leaders to the Boot Camp and in return you'll receive men and women who are stronger leaders. They'll be transformed into effective managers who energize their teams, enable their people to see a clear relationship between their daily duties and organizational goals, communicate a consistent leadership philosophy throughout the organization, and instill smart work strategies in their team to achieve tangible results.

The Lead2Succeed Process™:
Creating Great Leaders and Sound Strategies
from the Top Down

Most managers are technically competent but often lack the ability to motivate and direct others to achieve organizational goals. The Lead2Succeed Process helps solve this problem by converting managers into leaders who:

- Seek responsibility.
- Hold themselves accountable for their own actions.
- Train their people as a team.
- Make sound and timely decisions.
- Communicate effectively.
- Plan for success.
- Create a positive, enthusiastic, and supportive environment in which their team members can be successful.

There are four distinct components—Leadership Assessment, Focus & Alignment Workshop, Application and Action Sessions, and Evaluation and Follow-up:

- **Leadership Assessment:** Identify what types of activities energize great leaders and what activities energize or frustrate team members.
- **Focus & Alignment Workshop:** Determine the *purpose, values, vision, mission,* and *goals* that will guide your company into the future and provide the common thread for developing leaders.
- **Application and Action Sessions:** Take part in the training and application of selected leadership topics. These sessions help participants create a common "leadership language" and enable those at each level to coach and mentor others as they undergo the program.
- **Evaluation and Follow-up:** Learn to use periodic measurements and reports to determine the progress being achieved in individual skill development and the overall program goals.

Our program is designed to achieve results based on your company's specified goals. Lead2Succeed helps your organization achieve company goals, inspires employees to take initiative in indentifying and completing tasks, fosters better communication from the top down to the bottom up, and motivates employees to give their best every day.

The Vision-Based Strategic Planning Process

Where will your organization be in 10, 20, or 30 years—on the *Fortune* 500 list or out of business? To know if you are succeeding as an organization, you have to know where you are headed. This six-day intensive, interactive workshop helps you and your team create your company's vision and the strategic plan that will help you achieve it.

In addition to the preparation of the vision and strategic plan, we also work with you and your team to develop a systems view of your organization. This enables you to consider options for improving your organizational and management structures and improve your overall business focus and performance. And since changing your corporate culture is often a critical part of the plan, we also incorporate processes for accomplishing that in the workshop, and develop strategies to continue it.

Our proven Vision-Based Planning Process creates for you and your team:

- A vision that is truly shared by all your leadership.
- Clearly defined top-level goals by which to achieve your vision.
- Clearly defined, quantitative objectives by which to achieve the goals.
- Strategies by which to achieve each objective, including strategies for cultural change.
- Action steps by which to accomplish each strategy.

- Implementation plan.
- Metrics—MOEs and MOPs.
- Assigned roles and responsibilities.
- Stakeholder strategies for gaining and keeping their support.
- A War Room report providing the logic trail.

At the end of the planning process, you'll have a vision that is shared by all your leadership, clearly defined top-level goals, strategies for achieving them, a strong, cohesive team, and much more.

Lessons from the Battlefields: Academy Leadership Experiences Explore the Past to Help You Create a Better Future

The Gettysburg Leadership Experience. An excellent opportunity to gain a deeper understanding of leadership, teamwork, and communication, the Gettysburg Leadership Experience brings senior executive teams to the site of the greatest battle ever fought in North America. Through on-the-ground study of the leadership challenges faced by the commanders in this pivotal battle of the American Civil War, participants learn practical, usable lessons that will benefit their organizations today and beyond. Participants gain new insights and new ideas on:

- How leaders can make the right calls amid murky, ill-defined conditions, incomplete information, and high pressure.
- The intricacies of decision making and communication in very large organizations, and how culture affects what's possible.
- How successful leaders share their vision for success, reduce the possibility of misinterpretation, and get everyone pulling in the same direction.
- How leaders develop imagination and courage in themselves and others.
- Why character, a central element of leadership, is the key to building trust on teams.

Our experienced team of leader-facilitators uses stories of key leadership moments to bring critical lessons to life in vivid detail. These lessons, in turn, render valuable insights into how successful leaders operate today.

Modeled on the U.S. Army Staff Ride, a technique used to train officers in leadership and decision making, the experience lets participants see and feel, as no history book or mere lecture can, the challenges commanders faced during these three pivotal days in our nation's history. Instructors provide the historical background and facilitate in-depth discussion to reach a deep understanding of "leadership in action." Executives leave excited about their opportunities to be better leaders and armed with battle-tested tools they can use immediately.

The Normandy Leadership Experience. Learn how to lead at the site of one of the world's great military operations—the 1944 Allied liberation of France. During the four-day program, you'll see and feel the challenges that were faced by commanders in WWII's pivotal battle. Instructors illustrate "leadership in action" by facilitating in-depth discussion on topics such as the strong character of Dwight Eisenhower and how it kept the allies working together, how exceptional leadership led to the victory of Pegasus Bridge, and how leaders kept their soldiers moving forward in the face of adversity on Omaha Beach. During this one-of-a-kind learning opportunity, you'll gain new insights and new ideas on how to:

- Build flexible organizations that carry on in the midst of chaos and rapid change.
- Develop leaders who are creative thinkers.
- Communicate strategic intent so that everyone understands and takes responsibility for the mission.
- Earn the trust of subordinates.
- Build strong coalitions, across cultures and generations, for competition in the global marketplace.
- Prepare the next generation of leaders.

Best of all, you'll leave the experience armed with battle-tested tools you can use immediately.

The American Revolution Leadership Experience: Concord Bridge. In the Concord Leadership Experience, executives visit the Minute Man National Historic site near Concord, Massachusetts, flashpoint of the American Revolution, to learn timeless lessons on leadership that can invigorate today's businesses. During a visit to the site of this 1775 day-long battle, participants learn practical, usable lessons about team building, morale and courage, dealing with ambiguity, effective communication, and the execution of strategic intent. These powerful tools will help leaders to energize their organizations and get them moving towards their business goals.

As with our other on-the-ground leadership experiences, walking this historic ground creates a learning atmosphere that is almost impossible to create in a conference room, because the experience, like leadership, is emotional as well as intellectual. Executives gain new insights and new ideas on:

- How leaders help the organization combat fear and uncertainty.
- The intricacies of contingency planning and war-gaming.
- How an organization's culture can be predictive of performance.
- How leaders influence morale.
- How leaders organize effective teams.

Participants leave ready to meet the challenges of leading in today's complicated business world head on.

Out of the Trenches:
Inspirational Leadership Messages to Help Improve Your Organization

Are you looking for that perfect speaker or perfect subject for an annual company dinner, a professional association, or part of a larger event? The Academy Leadership staff has experience in speaking on a variety of leadership topics, such as leadership philosophy, productivity improvement, how to motivate people, how to manage conflict, how to develop future leaders, and more.

We can tailor a presentation to your audience and your specific needs. Whether you choose a keynote speech or one of our workshops, our programs will allow you to apply leadership principles to your organization's current situation. Your next company dinner could be the perfect opportunity to share valuable lessons in leadership with your staff.

Lead the Way Today!

If you would like to take part in one of Academy Leadership's results-driven workshops or training programs, or if you would like to book one of our speakers for your next company event, visit www.academyleadership.com or call us at 610-783-0630.

BOOKS FROM ACADEMY LEADERSHIP PUBLISHING

The Core Values Compass: Moving from Cynicism to a Core Values Culture
(2010, ISBN: 978-0-9727323-5-2, $24.95)
by Dennis F. Haley

The Corporate Compass: Providing Focus and Alignment to Stay the Course, 2nd Edition
(2009, ISBN: 978-0-9727323-6-9, $24.95)
by Ed Ruggero and Dennis F. Haley

The Leader's Compass: A Personal Leadership Philosophy Is Your Key to Success, 2nd Edition
(2005, ISBN: 978-0-9727323-1-4, $24.95)
by Ed Ruggero and Dennis F. Haley

Inspiring Leadership: Character and Ethics Matter
(2004, ISBN: 978-0-9727323-2-1, $24.95)
by R. Stewart Fisher and Perry J. Martini

Academy Leadership books are available at special quantity discounts to use as premiums and sales promotions, or for use in corporate training programs. For more information, please call Academy Leadership at 866-783-0630, visit www.academyleadership.com, or write to: 10120 Valley Forge Circle, King of Prussia, PA 19406.